WHO KILLED DR BOGLE AND MRS CHANDLER?

This paperback edition published in 2017 by New Holland Publishers
London • Sydney • Auckland

The Chandlery, 50 Westminster Bridge Road, London SE1 7QY, United Kingdom
1/66 Gibbes Street, Chatswood, NSW 2067, Australia
5/39 Woodside Ave, Northcote, Auckland 0627, New Zealand

newhollandpublishers.com

First edition published in 2012

A record of this book is held at the British Library and the National Library of Australia.

ISBN 9781742576411

Group Managing Director: Fiona Schultz
Publisher: Alan Whiticker
Project Editor: Jodi De Vantier
Proof Reader: Meryl Potter
Internal Designer: Stephanie Foti
Cover Designer: Lorena Susak
Production Director: James Mills-Hicks
Printer: Hang Tai Printing Company Limited.

This project has been kindly assisted by Screen Australia

10 9 8 7 6 5 4 3 2 1

Keep up with New Holland Publishers on Facebook
facebook.com/NewHollandPublishers

WHO KILLED DR BOGLE AND MRS CHANDLER?

PETER BUTT

CONTENTS

Acknowledgements

For their wonderful assistance over my six-year journey, I am indebted to many people.

I owe special thanks to my forensic referee, Tom Milby MD, for travelling half way round the world at his own expense to visit the 'crime scene' and review my discoveries; and to the late Geoffrey Chandler, who, without reservation or restriction, allowed me to delve into the darkest chapters of his life.

Thanks are also due to the NSW Police for providing me access to the scientific documents related to the case; and to former detective Ron Rudgley, who wrote the excellent final police report on the case and reviewed my manuscript, as well as to former scientific detective George Lindsay, who supplied photographs and rich memories of the events of New Year's Day 1963.

Toxicologist Vivian Mahoney and maritime scientist Maurice Fry are owed tremendous gratitude for their individual recall in vivid detail of their respective scientific investigations all those years ago—investigations that together resulted in producing the vital missing pieces in this extraordinary puzzle.

I must thank Professor Jo Duflou for writing his Foreword and for being ever generous with his time, good humour and vigorous interrogation of my work.

Thanks also to Film Australia—now Screen Australia—for backing my original research and providing access to interviews, photographs and movie footage for the eBook version of this work; and to Anna Grieve, Kris Wyld, Calvin Gardiner, Beverley Freeman, the production crew and the many actors who brought the Bogle-Chandler story to life on film.

Finally, for her critical and insightful reading of the manuscript, as well as her encouragement, forbearance and love, I am forever indebted to my dear wife, Sarah Staveley.

Foreword

Would the deaths of Dr Bogle and Mrs Chandler been solved if today's forensic science techniques had been available in the early 1960s? You would hope the answer is in the affirmative, but in reality I'm not too sure. Contemporary forensic science includes a vast array of applied technology and scientific endeavour, including the areas of molecular biology, advanced toxicological techniques, immuno-assays, robotic systems, and computerised imaging to name a few. In some ways, television shows such as *CSI* and *NCIS* are the greatest prime-time ads for forensic science. Complex plots, photogenic and witty characters, high tech equipment and outstanding detective work combine to get their man.

In fact, real life forensic science is more often reflected in the genre typified by the *X-Files*, complete with conspiracy theory, uncertainty, doubt and multiple theories, many of which are simply outrageous. Technology invariably plays a support role to the investigative skills of numerous groups of people, and complex cases can take months, if not years, of hard work to solve. If lucky, the case is taken to court, either the Coroner's Court or the various criminal courts, where the case is lost or won. To the jury member, the expert in the witness box must be a strange creature, and definitely very different to the heroic television forensic scientist. The alleged expert invariably does not express certainty, but rather presents evidence peppered with 'I don't know', 'I can't tell', 'I'm not sure', 'maybe' and 'possibly'. Surely the scientist is incompetent and evasive? In fact, the chances are no—what the scientist is trying to explain is the uncertainty that pervades all aspects of forensic science, and it is invariably the confident and definite forensic scientist who has a poor appreciation of the limitations of their work. So is this any different to the 1960s? Probably yes, but above all else, forensic scientists have become more cognisant of the fallibility and uncertainty inherent in their techniques, and they express their doubt more clearly.

The investigation of death scenes has progressed by leaps and bounds. What was often a haphazard and quick look-over by a police scientific officer now can involve multiple experts attending in sequential fashion, each adding their expertise to the investigation. Simple suspicious death scenes commonly take 12 hours or longer to process, and some can take whole teams of investigators many days at the location alone. The autopsy, similarly, can easily take an entire day to perform the basic investigations, followed by months of additional investigations including toxicology, molecular biology (or DNA) and other esoteric investigations. But the process has remained roughly the same over the last half century—forensic scientists investigating a death, using relatively limited technological assistance. In most suspicious deaths, the cause of death is obvious, be it a shooting, stabbing, poisoning or strangulation. Possibly with the exception of DNA testing, if the investigator has to rely on esoteric science for an answer, the chances are that answer will not be found.

But what about the deaths of Bogle and Chandler specifically? The scene appeared straightforward: two dead lovers at the side of a river. There was minimal physical evidence to retrieve, and documentation was easy. There were only minor injuries to both persons, and these were consistent with crawling on the undergrowth. Therefore, the method whereby they died must surely have been poisoning. It would be hard to realistically consider any other method, but it always pays to keep an open mind. The autopsies were essentially negative—characteristic of a poisoning death. Relevant specimens were sent to the analyst for detection of drugs and poisons, but this, of course, is where the whole investigation collapsed. There were simply no drugs, no poisons. For that matter, there were also no communist death rays, lasers, crocodile bile, or the myriad other bizarre and pure fantastical theories. The causes of death of both Dr Bogle and Mrs Chandler, no matter how hard investigators tried, stubbornly remained 'Undetermined'. This is not how it is meant to happen in *CSI*, where everything is always solved, certainty is achieved, and no questions remain unanswered, all in 60 minutes (including 12 or more minutes of ads).

Had Bogle and Chandler died today, the scene

would no doubt have been examined and documented in greater detail. Maybe additional evidence would have been uncovered, but I doubt it. The autopsies would likely have been conducted over a longer period of time. Probably nothing obvious would have been found, although maybe someone would have commented that the bodies appeared to be decomposing a bit faster than expected. Or maybe not. Toxicology would, in all likelihood, have come up with similar negative results. Unless you know what you're looking for, you're unlikely to find it, even if it is right in front of your eyes. Today, there would no doubt have been extensive DNA testing, phone taps and many other modern investigative techniques. Despite all of this though, I suspect the cases would have inexorably moved in the direction of 'Undetermined' yet again. There simply is no cause of death.

So what would happen next? Sooner or later, there would be an inquest. No doubt, it would have made the news today as well. Although many things have changed in the last half-century, and the Sydney of the 1960s described by Peter Butt in this book is very different to the Sydney of today, many things have also remained the same. There's still the excitement of salacious sex, mystery, people with things to hide and, above all else, two deaths of undetermined causes. This was grist for the mill for the media of the 1960s, and not much has changed. You only have to look at the daily revelations and publicity reported in the media in the more recent Dianne Brimble case to appreciate this.

With all the publicity would come the unsolicited

advice from 'experts' in the field, as well as from interested and well-meaning members of the public. Whenever an unsolved case hits the news, investigators including the police, the Coroner and forensic scientist get emails, letters and phone calls with suggestions from the general public. Most of these ideas are simply not supported by the evidence, and they are rapidly cast aside. However, every so often someone comes up with a really good lead which no-one had thought of before. The case is being looked at using a new approach, unencumbered by pre-conceived ideas, and sometimes those ideas really are novel and worth serious consideration. Professional forensic scientists and investigators, despite what they may secretly hope, do not have a monopoly on solving forensic science mysteries. Besides the inevitable problem of 'institutional straight-jacketing', most workers in the field juggle dozens if not hundreds of cases at any one time, and frustratingly difficult cases often don't get the time and resources they should. On the other hand, that enthusiastic member of the public for whom the case becomes a passion and an obsession, has the time, the mental resources and that unencumbered new approach to tackle this unsolvable mystery.

Peter Butt is one of those rare members of the public who has had genuine new insights into these puzzling deaths, and he has now written the story of his investigation into the deaths of Dr Bogle and Mrs Chandler. His tale is not a flash in the pan—what follows is a detailed investigation of the puzzling deaths of two people that has stymied every other person who has taken on the investigation. No other person has spent as much time studying these deaths and the associated cultural norms of Sydney in the 1960s. This is a great read if considered purely from the perspective of a description of Australian society in the early sixties, but of course it is much more than that. It describes the difficulties experienced by police and forensic investigators, often the consequences of political interference and the confounding effects of the social mores of the day. He has unearthed new information through persistent inquiry, and he has realised the significance of previously overlooked critical information. His scientific investigation and explanations are well thought out and are entirely reasonable and plausible, to the extent that I'm sure I was heard to mutter 'I wish I'd thought of that' on a number of occasions. For that matter, on those occasions where I have challenged Peter in relation to the science over the years, he has come back with answers, bolstering his argument further.

Has the mystery which has defeated professional forensic scientists for almost 50 years finally been solved by a determined and enthusiastic amateur? I don't know, but if it hasn't been, surely this must be the most detailed and well-considered investigation ever on the deaths of Dr Bogle and Mrs Chandler to date.

Jo Duflou
Chief Forensic Pathologist
Clinical Professor, University of Sydney

Introduction

As a schoolboy growing up Australia in the 1960s, I was both gripped and unsettled by a spate of home-grown mysteries, including the disappearance of the Beaumont children, the Wanda Beach murders and the bizarre disappearance of Prime Minister Harold Holt.

The story that had the most impact on my youthful imaginings was the infamous Bogle-Chandler case. With no clues as to how they died, the half-naked bodies of brilliant physicist Dr Gilbert Bogle and Mrs Margaret Chandler were found beside the Lane Cove River on New Year's Day, 1963. Adding to the mystery was the strange manner in which their bodies were covered.

The place where they died was a ten-minute drive from my family home. My father, a qualified pest controller, frequently treated trees along the river for termites. When the NSW Police announced that it was believed the couple had been poisoned, I even wondered whether my father's work had something do with the deaths. Our back shed was a poisoner's apothecary!

The story continued to interest me throughout adulthood. I devoured everything written about the case and watched scores of new theories come and go. It was simply incredible that the police could not determine how these two healthy people had died. Even more extraordinary was that the perpetrator, if there was one, had left no evidence.

In late 2004, some twenty-five years into my career as a documentary filmmaker, I decided to do a little digging of my own. What could I find out about this case that was new? Two of my previous films about Australia's secret nuclear history involved trawling through declassified top-secret government documents, so that was where I decided to start.

Within a few days, I had uncovered a file detailing a joint Military Intelligence/Commonwealth Police investigation into the prime suspect in the Bogle-Chandler case, Geoffrey Chandler. The investigators wanted to know whether or not Chandler had had access to chemical weapons at a laboratory in Melbourne. The fact that Australia was not officially carrying out chemical weapons research at the time made the document even more compelling.

My next step was to find Geoffrey Chandler, to see if he knew of the investigation. After a few frustrating weeks, I located the reclusive 74-year-old, who was living in country New South Wales. By chance, he was coming to Sydney and offered to meet up on neutral ground. When the inner city café I had chosen proved too noisy, I suggested we go to my home, where he settled in and then asked if he could stay a night or two. We got on well. Both of us had studied electronics and saw the world through a scientific prism. Three days into his stay, I finally mustered up the courage to broach the delicate subject of his wife's death. Chandler told me he had lived with the nightmare for four decades and the accusations that he was the culprit had never ceased. The worst experience, he said, was a woman turning up at his front door in answer to an advertisement for a live-in child-minder. She didn't want the job. She said she merely wanted to see what a murderer looked like.

When I finally handed Chandler the file he was gobsmacked. He admitted working in Melbourne for a year or so, but in electronics not chemical weapons research. After four days together, as we set off for the railway station, he pondered on what else I could find out about his wife's mysterious death. Chandler said he would back me all the way, even offering money, which I declined.

Twelve months later I contacted Geoffrey Chandler to say that I might have discovered what killed his wife and his colleague Dr Bogle and that the Deputy Commissioner of Police had granted me unprecedented access to the scientific aspects of the case files to continue my research. In 2006, I presented my discoveries on ABC television to the largest audience for a documentary in the broadcaster's fifty-year television history.

This book, based on a further four years of research, takes the story well beyond the scope of the film. It presents detailed evidence missed by the original investigators identifying what killed the victims, numerous similar cases from around the world and remarkable testimonies of people who observed the killer's presence at the river.

It also provides new revelations regarding the identity of the person who covered the bodies, how one of the key players in the story was an ASIO agent and the mysterious contents of an FBI file on the case.

I felt it important to reveal the reasons why both the original investigation and the Coronial Inquest failed the victims. It involved the suppression of evidence concerning the private worlds of Dr Bogle and Mrs Chandler. Some of that evidence is presented here—not for prurient reasons—but to finally make sense of why they ended up dead on the bank of Lane Cove River on New Year's Day, 1963.

Peter Butt, Sydney

1. New Year's Day

With its siren wailing, the NSW police-issue Studebaker Lark pulled out across the Pacific Highway against a red light. Working the morning shift on New Year's Day in Sydney, Sergeant Arthur Andrews and Senior Constable Nicholls had drawn the short straw. It was just after 10 am and unlike their colleagues, who were likely still sleeping off their celebratory excesses, their job was to clean up the worst of what the dying hours of 1962 and the twitching hours of 1963 could muster.

Their vehicle sped down Millwood Avenue, past lifeless brick bungalows, around a long sweeping bend, until the Lane Cove River came into view. Beside Fullers Bridge, two grim-faced teenage boys waved the car around the corner to the entrance of the riverside track. The youths led the way. On the left, towering eucalypts clung to sandstone outcrops. To the right, she-oaks whistled in the gentle summer breeze and contorted mangroves crowded the muddy riverbed. Through the discord of vegetation, the river was dark and stagnant.

Like most Chatswood policemen, Andrews had routinely patrolled the secluded track looking for rubbish dumpers and voyeurs who stalked young lovers parked in their cars. This callout, however, sounded far more serious. Eighty-two metres along, on a grassy verge by the riverbank, lay a man in a dark-grey suit, on his stomach. Nicholls ushered the boys back as Andrews inspected the lifeless body. The man's face, turned side-on, had a blue-purple hue and dry bloodstained mucus below his right nostril. A relatively fresh patch of vomit lay a few inches away. Andrews knelt and gingerly lifted the man's wrist. The skin was cold to touch. There was no pulse.

Fifteen-year-old Michael McCormick said he had taken the bush track at around 8.30 to meet a friend at the Chatswood Golf Links to collect golf balls. It was then that he first saw the man lying there. He thought the fellow was merely drunk and had passed out. An hour or so later, McCormick and his friend, Denis Wheway, returned along the track. The man hadn't moved and his lips and face had turned purple. They went for help, stopping a moment on the bridge to look for fish. Proprietor of the park kiosk, Geoffrey Little, followed them back. A war veteran, Little said he had seen plenty of dead men and this fellow certainly looked dead. Little hurried back to his kiosk and called the police.

Andrews walked around the body. There was something peculiar about the clothing. The suit was only draped over the man giving the impression he was dressed. Peeling off the coat, there was something even more curious—a rectangular portion of dirty-brown carpet lying on top of his shirt. Lifting off the trousers, the man was naked from the waist down, except for his socks and muddied shoes.

Andrews turned the body onto its side. It was semi-rigid. He looked for signs of injury, but there was nothing to suggest he had met with a violent death.

Nicholls radioed for assistance. Ten minutes later, three more policemen arrived, including Detective Sergeant Henry Parsons, who ran a team of over two-dozen detectives.

Parsons inspected the wallet taken from the dead man's coat pocket, and then returned to Chatswood Police Station to make enquiries, leaving instructions with his men to search the area for evidence.

If the state of the man's clothing wasn't puzzling enough, the riverside location was to deliver yet another surprise. Searching downstream, in the direction of the golf links, a constable came across an unusual array of flattened-out beer cartons on the muddy riverbed.

On closer inspection, he noticed a human leg protruding slightly from beneath the cardboard.

'There's another one down here!' he yelled.

Re-enactment

Andrews lifted the cartons, revealing the lifeless face of a pretty woman in her late 20s, lying on her back. Her clothing was in disarray. Both her rose-patterned, white dress and half-slip were gathered up, exposing the lower half of her body. The shoulder straps of the dress were down at her waist, along with her bra. Her slip, knees and bare feet were stained with black mud. At her feet lay a pair of men's jockey style underpants, wet and stained with excreta. It was an incongruous sight—a pretty woman in a white party dress amongst all that mud, reeking of faeces.

Following a radio message, Parsons returned to the crime scene and slid down the grass-covered bank. He lifted the victim's hand to check for a pulse. There was none.

'Still warm', he half-whispered.

Again, there were no obvious external signs to suggest how the victim had died. There was also nothing to identify the woman—no handbag or purse. She wore a simple wedding ring, but there was no inscription.

Parsons pondered the crime scene: two bodies less than 20 yards (18 metres) apart, a male on the grassy bank, a female on the exposed riverbed, both half naked and strangely covered, but no signs of violence.

A detective radioed the details to Criminal Investigation Branch (CIB) headquarters in the city. Across town, the newsrooms of the major dailies also picked up the transmission. The *Daily Mirror*'s Bill Jenkings was first at the scene. He reported:

> The first thing that struck me as the photographer and I trekked down through the bush to the river was the overpowering stench of death. I could smell and see human excreta and vomit. The stifling morning heat seemed to magnify the putrid odour.[1]

While the previous evening had been cool, it was turning out to be a typical hot Sydney New Year's Day. But the vagaries of the weather were not something that registered with the dozen detectives and uniformed policemen now traipsing the exposed riverbed for clues. They had what looked like a double murder on their hands and the tide was coming in.

Detective Sergeant Parsons and Constable Turner drove to Turramurra: a quiet, relatively new North Shore suburb about twenty minutes from Fullers Bridge. At the end of an unmade path shaded by gumtrees they came to a fashionable 1950s brick home. Vivienne Bogle appeared at the door with a baby in her arms.

With her four children and two relatives present, Parsons handed Mrs Bogle the wallet. It was in the pocket of a man, he said, found deceased beside the Lane Cove River. Papers inside bore the name of Dr Gilbert Stanley Bogle—a physicist with the CSIRO, the Commonwealth Scientific and Industrial Research Organisation.

Parsons encouraged Mrs Bogle to take a seat and then questioned her about Dr Bogle's recent movements. Fighting back tears, she said he had left home at 9 o'clock the previous evening to attend a New Year's Party at the home of a CSIRO colleague. At 5 am, when she awoke to attend to her crying baby, she became concerned that he had not returned home. At 6.45 am she telephoned the party hosts, Ken and Ruth Nash. Mrs Nash had said not to worry since it was a very late party and he hadn't long left. As the hours passed, she had become increasingly concerned, calling the police to see if he'd been in a car accident. Parsons said that it wasn't possible at this stage to determine what had happened to her husband.

What he had to say next was lodged in his throat; Vivienne Bogle was obviously an upright woman. He explained that there was another person found nearby and that she was also deceased.

From Parson's description of the woman, Mrs Bogle couldn't fathom who she was, let alone what she was doing with her husband.

Leaving the grief-stricken family, the detectives had little to go on beside the address of the New Year's party Bogle had attended. Fifteen minutes later, they walked up the path of a well-maintained liver-brick bungalow with a manicured English garden in Waratah Street, Chatswood. A short, nuggetty man with the creased face of a heavy smoker answered the door. Ken Nash confirmed that he and his wife had presided over a New Year's party and that Dr Gilbert Bogle was one of about twenty invited guests who had attended. Ruth Nash, a tall, attractive woman in her forties, appeared from the kitchen as her husband ushered the detectives into the sitting room, which was still in disarray, with half-empty glasses and overflowing ashtrays scattered all around.

Parsons explained that Dr Bogle had been found dead at the Lane Cove River. He asked the shocked hosts if a female wearing a rose-patterned dress had also attended the party.

Ruth Nash glanced to her husband. There had been a guest wearing a white summer frock with roses, she said. Mrs Margaret Chandler.

Re-enactment

Ken Nash recalled that Mrs Chandler had arrived at the party around 10.30 am with her husband Geoffrey, a fellow CSIRO colleague, and that she had left the party at about the same time as Dr Bogle, unaccompanied by her husband.

◆ ◆ ◆

Ravens passed over the bloated river as Parsons and Turner returned to the crime scene. In a dusty parking area beside Fullers Bridge, police officers were inspecting an old, khaki-coloured Ford Prefect. A registration check matched the car with the dead man. On the rear seat, they found a leather-covered case containing a clarinet and a surrealist Picasso-style, crayon sketch depicting a two-faced head and an assortment of severed limbs. Above the steering wheel, tucked behind the sun-visor, they found the key to the vehicle.

Meanwhile, sightseers had gathered on the bridge, trying to catch a glimpse of the police activity downstream where Scientific Investigation Branch detectives were now scouring the area for evidence.

On the exposed riverbed below Dr Bogle's body, scientific detective George Lindsay photographed a pair of ladies' panties, a man's belt, and a brown pair of ladies' court shoes. The items of apparel were spread out in a distinct line parallel to the riverbank.

Lindsay's senior colleague, Detective Sergeant Alan Clarke, ordered a couple of luckless policemen to collect human excreta both from the riverbed and the riverbank near Dr Bogle's body. Two police divers scrutinised the murky waterway, but agreed it offered too little visibility to search for evidence.

At 2 pm, the Government Medical Officer, Dr Brighton, arrived and examined both bodies. Pronouncing life extinct, he couldn't determine how either victim had died. Detectives then lifted Mrs Chandler's body from the riverbed and placed her face down onto newspapers spread across the sandy track.

Four decades on, George Lindsay recalled inspecting both victims' bodies:

> My main job was to search for bullet holes or knife marks or anything like that to determine if they'd been assaulted in some way. There were no marks of any distinction. I had no suspicions how they died. They were just two young bodies. We couldn't work out the cause of death.[2]

The reporters were all eager to leave the site. As newspaperman, Bill Jenkings put it, 'Everyone's guts were churning from the foul smell.' The 'vapours of Death', he suggested.

As a mortuary van headed for the City Morgue, a large dog breached the crime scene barricade, wandered along the riverbank, then bounded down onto the mudflats, oblivious to the drama that had just unfolded.

So began one of the longest homicide and forensic investigations in New South Wales history. The lives of the victims and everyone associated with them would soon come under intense police scrutiny. The mystery surrounding the deaths would spark a fierce newspaper war, challenge conservative society, split families, ruin careers, cause mental breakdowns and suicides and drive some people out of the country for good.

Little did anyone realise that a witness to the deaths was still present in the vicinity—a witness whose own story was intimately entwined with the fate of the victims.

2. Alibi

Geoffrey Chandler

Thud. Thud. Thud.

At one o'clock in the afternoon, New Year's Day, an insistent banging reverberated through a modest, timber-clad Croydon Park cottage. A tall red-headed man with an unkempt beard dragged himself from his bed, wandered into the bedroom opposite and picked up a crying nine-month-old boy from his cot. Opening the front door, he squinted in the bright sun, trying to make out the silhouetted figures in hats in front of him. They looked like detectives, he thought.

'Geoffrey Chandler?' said one of the detectives.

'Yes.'

A second child appeared from behind Chandler and held onto his leg.

'What time is it?' he grumbled.

'Is your wife home?'

'No.'

At 3 pm, the Burwood detectives delivered Chandler and his two children to Chatswood Police Station. Female Constable Taylor took the boys into her care as a detective ushered Chandler along a corridor. He had no idea what this was all about. He could only imagine that something had happened to his wife. Detective-Sergeant Parsons looked up from a newspaper as Chandler entered his office. Pointing to the seat opposite him, Parsons offered nothing in the way of pleasantries:

'Is your wife's name Margaret Olive Chandler?' he said flatly.

'Yes.'

'Can you tell me where your wife is?'

'I have no idea where she is.'

Parsons slid the afternoon edition of the *Daily Mirror* across the desk and pointed to a front-page headline: 'Scientist, Woman in Death Mystery'. The story named Dr Gilbert Bogle and Mrs Margaret Chandler as the victims. His own name appeared as the woman's husband, misspelled 'Jeffrey' Chandler, an experimental officer of the Division of Radio Physics, CSIRO.

In 2005, Geoffrey Chandler recalled Parsons' calculating method:

> By this time the newspaper had an edition out with some great splurge on the front page. He showed that to me quite sort of cold-bloodedly to gauge my reaction, I guess. I was very, very tired from not having much sleep the night before. It was quite clear that their first and foremost thought was that I was responsible for Margaret's death.[3]

Parsons' intuitive, penetrating questioning had delivered confessions from scores of men and women sitting in that same chair. Many of his conquests had received life sentences.

Parsons waited patiently for a reaction to the newspaper report. Turner sat nearby ready to take down his every word. Finally, Chandler placed the paper on the desk, removed a cigarette from a pack in his shirt pocket and lit it. Strangely, he showed no emotion at the news of his wife's death. Parsons checked the time on his watch and asked Chandler about his and Margaret's relationship with the physicist, Dr Bogle.

'Gib' Bogle, he said, had been a colleague at the CSIRO for a number of years. They worked in different departments on different floors. Occasionally, they would pass each other in the corridor and say hello. He claimed that Margaret first met Bogle ten days earlier at a CSIRO Christmas party held at the Radio Astronomy facility at Murraybank. They had spent some time talking. Later that night, they had all gone back to the home of Ken and Ruth Nash for drinks. At Dr Bogle's suggestion, Nash invited them to their New Year's party.

Asked if his wife had further contact with Dr Bogle after the Christmas party, Chandler said with certainty that the next time they met was at the New Year's party.

Parsons questioned Chandler on his and Margaret's movements before, during and after the New Year's party. The previous night, he said, they had left their two children at Margaret's parents' home in Granville and arrived at the party in Chatswood around 10.30 pm.

Pamela Logan

Casually dressed in slacks, shirtsleeves and sandals, he said he had felt uncomfortable. The other men were wearing suits and ties. Margaret, in her summer, rose-patterned dress looked pretty, but the other women were more conservatively dressed.

Chandler said that at around 11.30 pm he had told his wife that he was going to buy cigarettes and then left the party alone. Just before midnight he arrived at another New Year's party in Phoebe Street, Balmain. The host, Ken Buckley, a controversial left-wing Professor of Economics at Sydney University, was renowned for his wild parties.

Chandler found Buckley's bash to be the antithesis of the effete Chatswood soirée. In the garden, he eased up to Pamela Logan, a twenty-one-year-old Sydney University Psychology Department secretary.

At 1.30 am, he and Logan left the Balmain party, driving in separate cars to Logan's rented room in Darlington. Half an hour later, Chandler said, he left Miss Logan and returned to the Chatswood party, arriving as supper was served. After another hour or so he again left the party alone.

Chandler didn't appear to be hiding anything. On the contrary, he was open about his affair with Pamela Logan. He also admitted leaving Margaret at the party, not once but twice. The second time was just after 4 am—about an hour before his wife and Dr Bogle had met their deaths.

'Did you have an argument with your wife?' said Parsons.

'No. My wife was to go with Dr Bogle by arrangement with my wife.'

'What do you mean by an arrangement?'

'By this I mean they both wished to go home together and I felt no objection towards this. They were attracted to each other.'

'Attracted to each other? Has your wife previously gone home from parties by arrangement with yourself?'

'No, she hadn't done this before, but I had no objection to her going home with him and having intercourse with him if she wanted it, and he wanted to have it with her.'

The explanation confounded Parsons. Chandler then recalled his parting words to Dr Bogle:

'I said to Gib, "Tell Margaret not to worry. I'll pick up the children from her parents' home".'

Chandler explained that he then drove across the Harbour Bridge and returned to Pamela Logan's bedsitter. A little while later they set off together to his wife's parents' home in Granville to pick up his children.

Parsons scribbled on his note pad: Chandler takes girlfriend to in-law's house!

To test Chandler's extraordinary alibi, Parsons drove to the south side of the city. At 4.20 pm a striking young woman, soft-featured with her blonde hair in a ponytail, came to the door of a Darlington Road terrace. Even in a housedress, Pamela Logan projected sophistication beyond her twenty-one years. Little did she realise that the doorbell had sounded the beginning of a bruising heavyweight bout that would batter her previously untarnished public reputation.

On presenting his identification, Parsons asked if Geoffrey Chandler had been in her company the previous evening and earlier that morning. Guardedly, Logan confirmed she had been with Chandler and questioned why they wanted to know.

Parsons evaded, saying only that Chandler had told them 'certain things' and suggested she could confirm them.

Logan reluctantly invited the detectives in. Seated at the kitchen table, she told them that Geoffrey had arrived at the Balmain party about midnight and that they left together about 1.30 am, driving in their own cars to her

Darlington bed-sitter. Half an hour later, Chandler had departed and she went to bed. At about 4.30 am she had been woken by a knock at the door. Chandler had returned. She was annoyed, she said, but he somehow cajoled her to go with him to pick up his children from his in-laws' home at Granville. As she dressed, she noticed that it was 5 am on her bedside clock.

On the journey to Granville, Chandler told her that he had deliberately arranged for Dr Bogle to take his wife home and expected them to have intercourse.

As they approached Granville, Chandler dropped her off on Parramatta Road while he went to collect two-year-old Gareth and nine-month-old Sean. On the return journey, their car ran out of petrol. Three young men offered assistance and they finally arrived back at her home about 6 am, where Chandler and the children remained until 10 am.

As incredible as Logan's account sounded, it neatly matched Geoffrey Chandler's version of events.

Logan pressed Parsons to explain what had happened, insisting that she was not about to answer any further questions without a lawyer. Using a powerful tactic designed to terrify young people and goad them into cooperating, Parsons asked where her parents were. They lived in Sydney, she said, but refused to divulge their address.

Parsons asked if she knew Geoffrey Chandler was married and whether or not Mrs Chandler knew about her. Logan demanded to know what that had to do with anything. Parsons contemplated the young, frightened woman then leaned forward, 'Do you know that Mrs

Chandler and a Dr Gilbert Bogle were found dead this morning?'

Pamela Logan immediately burst into tears. There appeared to be nothing artificial about her reaction.

◆ ◆ ◆

On his return to Chatswood Police Station, Parsons briefed Detective Inspector Watson, who was sent across from CIB headquarters to head the murder investigation. In his opinion, the person of most interest, Geoffrey Chandler, appeared to have an alibi. At dawn, when Dr Bogle and his wife were at the Lane Cove River, Chandler had been on the other side of the city with his pretty young lover who had corroborated every detail of his story.

At 9 pm, Parsons and Watson started questioning Chandler all over again, both for the benefit of obtaining a signed, typewritten statement and to test Chandler for consistency.

Watson probed him about his relationship with his wife. Chandler claimed that he and Margaret had a happy marriage. But he also had no problem with her taking a lover, as he believed it would be 'transitory'. To prove his point, he said Margaret had previously had an affair with a friend of his, both with his knowledge and approval. He claimed that it had no negative impact at all on his marriage and only enhanced it. Even for the world-weary detectives, such a liberal attitude was incomprehensible.

As the grilling continued, Chandler sensed that he remained their prime suspect:

> They were convinced that I was the killer, and they did everything they could to sort of prove that that was the case. They didn't use any overt physical force, but there was an awful lot of covert intimidation, like the big burly copper with a gun on his belt standing alongside my ear. I just went into a state of tight internal control where the purpose was to survive this scene with the police.[4]

The interview ended at 2 am, thirteen arduous hours after Chandler had opened his door to the detectives. At this stage, there was nothing to connect him to the riverside deaths of his wife and Dr Gilbert Bogle. Yet his extraordinarily cool, unemotional testimony did nothing to allay suspicions. If Geoffrey Chandler was a double-murderer, he was certainly a clever one.

3. The Victims

Dr Gilbert Bogle

In the police yard the following morning, scientific detectives scoured Dr Bogle's car for evidence, collecting sweepings from the interior and the boot and swabs of the door handles. Meanwhile, the heavyweights from CIB and a dozen detectives from 4th and 25th Division were crowded into a room at the rear of the building for a briefing. Parsons ran through the basic facts. Two bodies, no obvious cause of death, but the autopsies would hopefully give them something to go on soon. Parsons then handed over proceedings to Detective Inspector Watson, the CIB Officer in charge of the investigation.

While they waited for conclusive scientific evidence, Watson told them to keep an open mind as to who was responsible. Murder was the most likely scenario. But their logical suspect at this time, Geoffrey Chandler, had provided a watertight alibi, which was backed up by his lover, Pamela Logan.

Aside from murder, they had to consider all other means by which these two people, with such youth, promise and family responsibilities, could have met their end. Double-suicide seemed unlikely, as the victims had only met once prior to their deaths. Murder-suicide, Watson said, could not be ruled out, particularly if one of the victims was suffering some form of psychosis.

The local detectives knew that the Lane Cove River was a popular transit zone for people planning to take their own life. In 1903, 43-year-old labourer Thomas McIvor destroyed his personal papers, said his prayers, read his Bible a little, then went down to the river and killed himself by jumping off a wharf. Stephen Trickett, a 24-year-old Narromine Shire Clerk, who was suffering ill health, travelled to Sydney in February 1915 and drowned himself. In 1921, a coroner found that 19-year-old domestic servant Alice Hanagan had wilfully submerged herself in the waters of Lane Cove River and drowned. And in 1947, local resident Hilda Fletcher drowned herself following a nervous breakdown.

While neither Bogle nor Chandler had drowned, Watson set his detectives the task of finding out as much as possible about the lives of both victims.

Perhaps there was something in their backgrounds or mental makeup to explain how he or she ended up half-naked and dead beside the Lane Cove River.

Dr Bogle in his laboratory

Born in Wanganui, New Zealand on 5 January 1924, Gilbert Stanley Bogle studied physics at Victoria University College during World War II. Awarded a Rhodes scholarship in 1947, he moved to Britain, where he studied for his degree of Doctor of Philosophy at Oxford University, graduating in 1949 with First Class Honours. In September 1950, at the Great Dunmow parish church, in Essex, Bogle married schoolteacher Vivienne Mary Rich, a fellow graduate of Victoria University, and daughter of the Anglican Bishop of Wellington.[5]

The Bogles returned to New Zealand in 1952, where Gilbert took up a position at the University of Otago, researching and lecturing in physics. In October

1955, with three young children and frustrated by the limitations of research at the university, Bogle applied for a position in Australia with the CSIRO. A senior university colleague provided a glowing personal and professional reference: 'He is both socially and scientifically a most refreshing person, and he certainly would be a great asset to any laboratory.'[6]

In late August 1956, the Bogle family departed Wellington on the elegant, celebrity steamship *Monowai*, bound for Australia. Five days later, they arrived in Sydney. In his new position at the CSIRO's National Standards Laboratory in the Radio Physics Building at Sydney University, Bogle quickly made an impression: 'Dr Bogle is noteworthy for his mental powers, his breadth of knowledge, his capacity for original ideas, his drive and enthusiasm, his range of experimental techniques and his outstanding ability as a lecturer.'[7]

Bogle's field of research centred on a revolutionary microwave amplifier called the Ruby Maser, which would have a great impact on both communications and radioastronomy, including the search for extraterrestrial life. After hours, his life revolved around tennis, hockey and singing in a local choir. An unnamed friend of Bogle told the *Sun*:

> Working, swimming, dancing or just talking, painting or playing the clarinet, explaining something to his children, just walking into a crowded room, he was—I use the word because I cannot think of one better—he was in everything, a beautiful man.[8]

Inquiries of his CSIRO chief revealed that Bogle had recently given notice. In a matter of weeks, he and his family were to be heading to the United States, where he had accepted a position with the preeminent science and technology corporation, Bell Laboratories. He said Bogle was excited by the prospect and had everything to live for. He was not the sort of person anyone could conceivably believe to be capable of taking his own life and that of another person.

◆ ◆ ◆

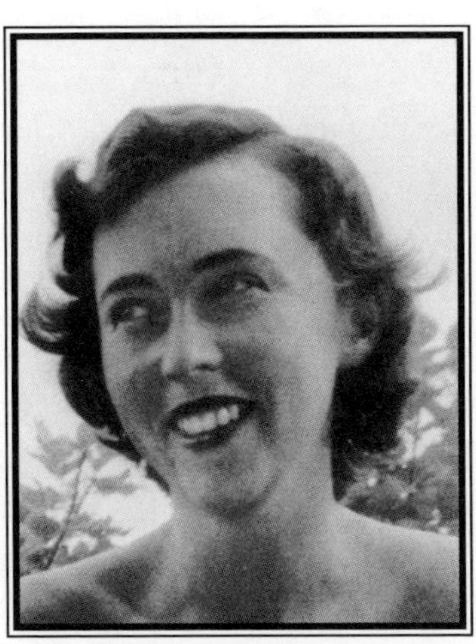

Margaret Chandler

On 2 April 1934, Margaret Morphett was born to textile executive Melville Morphett and his wife Olive. In 1952, after attending school at the sedate Presbyterian Ladies College in Croydon, she embarked on a nursing career at Royal Prince Alfred Hospital. According to her friends Margaret strove to be different from her conservative bobby-socked and pleated-skirt contemporaries.

Together with a girlfriend, she purchased a second-hand surfboard, took up hitchhiking, and on days off whiled away the hours on the beach with boys. In her late teens, she met a young Middle Eastern man. After dating on and off for two years, it became evident that cultural and religious differences precluded something permanent and Margaret ended the relationship. After completing her nursing training, Margaret 'specialled' at a private hospital.

On a freezing winter's evening in 1956, Margaret dined at a Kings Cross restaurant with her older brother, Tony, who introduced her to an acquaintance seated nearby—Geoffrey Chandler.

Chandler was immediately taken with the shy 22-year-old. Later that night, he ran into Margaret and Tony again at the newly opened El Rocco jazz venue at Kings Cross. By the end of the evening, according to Geoffrey Chandler, he and Margaret were growing comfortable together. He told her about his work in electronics for the CSIRO and how he restored vintage cars in his spare time. The following morning, her parents awoke to find a newcomer in their midst. They had spent the night tucked intimately under a rug on the lounge. Chandler stayed on for breakfast, lunch and dinner and, within a few weeks, was virtually living at the house. Margaret confided in a friend that she had never met anyone quite like him.

Geoffrey found Margaret, 'charming, demure, well-mannered and quiet. The warmth she emanated did not come from wit or out-going conversation. In those weeks, she was like someone with a special joyous secret, utter confidence in her own happy existence.'[9]

The Chandlers

The following year, Margaret fell pregnant. For both of them, there was no question of what to do. Chandler sensed that Margaret's parents would have preferred her to marry a professional man or a businessman. But the Morphetts realised she was very much in love with Geoffrey and accepted that it was her choice. They set a wedding date—Christmas Eve, 1957.

Two weeks before the wedding, Margaret miscarried. The wedding went ahead at St Stephen's Presbyterian Church, in Macquarie Street, Sydney, only a few blocks south of where toxicologists would soon be trying to determine how she met her death.

The couple purchased a modest weatherboard house in Croydon Park, in Sydney's western suburbs. Initially, life centred on restoring the house, vintage cars, dog breeding and trying to start a family.

Typical of men of his generation, Geoffrey Chandler regularly indulged in social activities without his wife. He also had affairs. But unlike most men, he made no secret of it. Moreover, he encouraged Margaret to take lovers.

In his interview with the police, Geoffrey Chandler suggested they talk with a friend of his, Bill Berry. Detectives traced Berry to Queensland. He explained how he and Geoffrey Chandler had first met at a party four years earlier in 1959. Some time later, Geoffrey had introduced him to Margaret and asked him to teach her to drive. After one driving lesson, Berry said they had intercourse, but was concerned Geoffrey would find out. Margaret said, 'He won't find out unless I tell him. Anyway, he goes off with other women.'

Berry claimed Geoffrey knew about the affair because he used to joke about it. But things became less jocular when Chandler returned home early from work one day to find the doors of his house locked. Through a window, he saw Margaret and Berry together. Chandler told Berry he was more upset about being locked out of his own house than finding him with his wife.

Bill Berry finally called off the affair with Margaret, because he was seeing another woman, who later became his wife.

In 2005 Berry's now ex-wife recalled:

> Bill Berry was my boyfriend. Yes, he had a brief affair with Margaret. She was a very sweet, lovable person and he was very sweet and lovable too. Geoff tended to feel

guilty that he had girlfriends, whereas Margaret didn't have boyfriends. So he encouraged my boyfriend of that time to have an affair with Margaret. Geoff told this to the police to give credence to his own lifestyle. But they just couldn't believe that anyone could have such an open marriage and not be jealous. They basically felt that Geoff would have been very jealous and that was his motive.[10]

Margaret and Geoffrey Chandler

Bill Berry told police Geoffrey Chandler was 'an easygoing fellow with a very placid nature' and not a jealous husband–type who would resort to murder.

Following Margaret's affair, and after more miscarriages, two babies came along in quick succession. But by late 1962, Margaret was trapped in suburbia. There was little in the way of social networks and she could go all day without talking to anyone.

Chandler's own observations about Margaret's last months were telling. He said that after the birth of their second child:

> Margaret became more a mother than a lover. She also neglected her post-natal exercises. She felt dull and inadequate, but was unable to correct it.[11]

A few days after her death, Geoffrey Chandler allegedly raised with her brother Tony the possibility that Margaret had committed suicide: 'I told Margaret she was inadequate for me. She was disturbed and probably did herself in.'

Friends and acquaintances of Margaret had noticed a marked decline in her frame of mind. Josephine Dabron, who first met Margaret a year before her death, sensed she was 'a very unhappy woman' because of Geoffrey Chandler's philandering. On a visit to the Chandler home, Dabron witnessed Margaret walking around the house crying. Two weeks before Margaret's death, Dabron again visited the Chandlers but was so incensed by Geoffrey's indifference to his wife that she walked out.

Detectives interviewed Margaret's local doctor. He described her as a good living, stable and intelligent person, but over time he had noticed her personal appearance deteriorate. The female proprietor of a Burwood dress store told police that Mrs Chandler came in before Christmas to buy a dress. During the fitting, she noticed that her clothes were soiled. But a week later, on 27 December, when Margaret returned to the store to buy another dress for the New Year's Eve party, her garments were clean. This transformation in her appearance and mood was clearly due to her meeting Dr Bogle at the Murraybank party. The following day Margaret told a friend:

> Don't take any notice of me. I am tired. We've been to the CSIRO Christmas party. I met a young fellow there and he paid me a lot of compliments and hung around. Doesn't it make you feel nice and young again?

Rather than suicidal, meeting the charismatic Bogle seemed to have rekindled Margaret's spirit and love of life. Geoffrey told the police that they had discussed the idea of Margaret taking Gib as a lover. Geoffrey agreed to her having an affair with Bogle if the opportunity arose. The detectives were mystified by this civilised negotiation of an extramarital affair. The victims they usually came across rarely had an opportunity to negotiate anything and the culprits invariably just took what they wanted.

From the evidence gathered, both Dr Bogle and Mrs Chandler were in positive frames of mind and looking forward to the New Year's party. How and why it all went cruelly wrong was still unfathomable. The police had found nothing to back either the double suicide or murder/suicide theories. Homicide still seemed the most likely solution.

4. Prime Suspect

At 9 am, after a fitful sleep, Chandler arrived at the City Morgue in Sydney's Rocks district. A uniformed policeman led him down a neon-lit corridor; the smell of bleach and formaldehyde failed to disguise the odours of death and decomposition. At another time, the CSIRO electronics engineer may have found himself peering through doors. It was just another laboratory, a little like his, and the human body merely a machine propelled by electrical impulses and controlled by a bio-computer.

Chandler was ushered into a stark viewing room to find his wife on a steel mortuary table covered in an over-starched, white sheet. A cabal of grim-looking detectives stood around the perimeter of the room, their eyes fixed on the tall, bearded husband.

Four decades later, Chandler recalled the scene:

> You couldn't possibly have conceived of a more callous way in which she was presented. In which they all arranged themselves to watch my every little action. To see whether I was going to break down. Whether I was going to confess. They were all standing around like ghouls, watching.[12]

Chandler stared at the mother of his two children; her hair peppered with bits of vegetation, a slight abrasion on the bridge of her nose, another on her right cheekbone, and at the top of both arms, similar scrape-abrasions. On her left hand, a wedding ring. She was only 28 years old. A rose.

'Mr Chandler, can you identify this person?' boomed a voice.

'She's a bit dishevelled, isn't she?' he said. 'She didn't have that mark on her nose.'

According to Ron Rudgley, a CIB detective who worked on the entire case, the investigators present were taken aback by Chandler's chilling response:

> He gave every indication of being completely blasé about his wife's death. He gave no indication that he was upset. He viewed the body and said, 'Oh she's a bit dishevelled, isn't she?' He certainly didn't show any emotion or great upset.[13]

Chandler sensed that the detectives were waiting for him to break down and confess:

> There was no overriding impression at all except of horror and a steely determination to not give in, to spite them all. They wanted me to collapse in a screaming heap. And I was not going to give them that satisfaction. [14]

Detective Ron Rudgley:

> Well, he was a suspect from day one. But we were in a

> situation where almost everything he told us could be supported by other evidence. The only thing that we had was a disparity of a few minutes between 4 am and 4.30 am. So there just wasn't any evidence to encourage our suspicion.

Despite his alibi, Geoffrey Chandler walked out of the City Morgue leaving many of the detectives even more convinced that he was the killer. That afternoon he went into hiding.

5. Autopsies

Government Analyst Laboratory

The post mortem examinations were carried out at 10.30 am and 11 am respectively on 2 January, immediately after the bodies were identified. The Director of the Division of Forensic Medicine, Dr Laing, estimated the time of death as between 24 to 36 hours earlier. Aside from superficial scratches on both bodies, there was no evidence of violence. Meticulous examinations for needle marks and spider bites came up negative. In both cases, Laing attributed death to 'acute cardiac failure associated with anoxia and pulmonary oedema'—meaning their hearts stopped and they ceased breathing, the order of which was unknown.

Dr Laing noted, 'The means by which the deaths had been effected could not be established.'

The only logical conclusion, he told the police, was that Dr Bogle and Mrs Chandler had been poisoned. To discover the identity of the poison, Laing dispatched the victims' organs, as well as swabs and smears, to the Government Analyst for chemical analyses and pathological examination.

The Government Analyst's Chief Toxicologist, Vivian Mahoney, was holidaying at his parents' home in Central Queensland when he heard the breaking news on the radio:

> I heard that two people had been found dead on the banks of the Lane Cove River. And I think the words were in 'tragic' or 'suspicious' circumstances. I had an idea at the time that I'd be spending a lot of time on that case when I returned to Sydney.[15]

The following day, Mahoney flew back to Sydney. The next morning, he drove from his Northbridge home across the Harbour Bridge and parked beneath the majestic 19th century sandstone Department of Health Building in Macquarie Street; a few blocks away from where the Sydney Opera House was under construction. When he walked into his laboratory, he was handed what was to become the longest and most personally distressing case of his twelve-year career. His boss, 'Sammy' Ogg, a balding chemist with thirty years experience in toxicology, briefed him on the autopsy reports: 'Well, there's nothing much of relevance there. Pulmonary oedema, anoxia, cyanosis—both had vomited and excreted.'

From Mahoney's experience, there was nothing unusual about the failure of a post-mortem examination to reveal the cause of death. He agreed that it looked like the victims had been poisoned:

> What happens at the autopsy is purely and simply a physical examination of the bodies. It indicates physically what has occurred in the body. If they can't conclude the cause of death—and they usually can't—they immediately send the parts of the body across for chemical analysis. In the case of Bogle and Chandler, I don't think there was any secret that poison was the initial assumption because they didn't meet their deaths physically. There was no physical evidence of being attacked. They weren't choked. They weren't shot. It was quite obvious it could only be one thing; something entered those two bodies. They had to have consumed something, inhaled something or absorbed something through the skin. So that's why we are called in to try and isolate this mystery poison from those organs. We generally get the stomach, liver, kidney, spleen, small intestine and some blood. They assume if there's any poison being taken, that's where it will end up.[16]

Mahoney took over the preparation of the victims' tissue samples. Preparation of the samples was crudely mechanical. A shiny butchers' mincer, a blender and various domestic pots and pans were his tools of trade. Analysis, however, would involve Bunsen burners and an impressive, twisted array of glassware bubbling with chemicals.

Toxicologist Viv Mahoney

As a sporting enthusiast, Mahoney usually only read the horse racing form guide and football news in the papers. He didn't see the photograph of himself and Mr Ogg in their 'crowded, makeshift, laboratory' and the accompanying story headed 'Test Tube Detectives'. It was deliberate. Mahoney didn't want to know anything about the victims or any speculation about how they died. Science would provide the truth, and if that truth was poison, then it had to lie in the victims' tissues. But just as Vivian Mahoney began his analysis, his lab assistant asked whether he recalled the name 'Bogle':

> Coincidentally, we'd met him at a symposium at Sydney University attended by scientists. It was at a morning break around the table having a cup of tea. It didn't register that it was Dr Bogle until my assistant pointed it out. I think he called him, 'the small fellow that was

> doing a lot of the talking'. That's the way he put it. He asked me, 'Do you remember him' and I said, 'Yes, I do remember him.'

Bogle had shaken Mahoney's hand that day. Now in Mahoney's hands was the responsibility of identifying what had killed the physicist. But Mahoney was not daunted: 'You've got to be very impersonal. Familiarity with the victim has to be put aside for the sake of scientific objectivity.'

In the Bogle-Chandler case, however, Mahoney's strategy was one that would come to haunt him.

6. A Room Full of Suspects

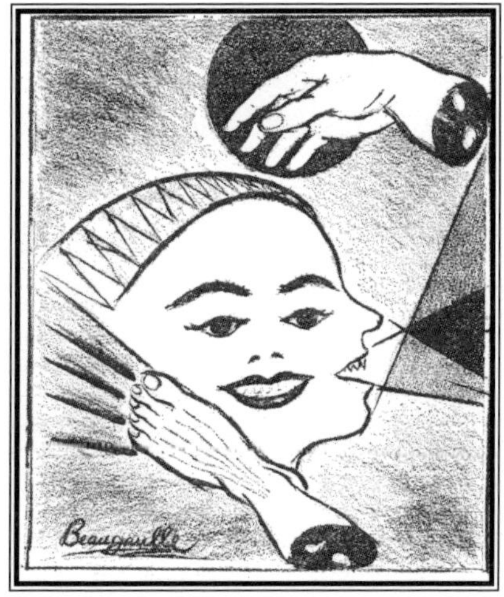

Dr Bogle's artwork

The police estimated the time of death to be between 5 and 5.30 am on New Year's morning. The first sighting of Dr Bogle's car at the Lane Cove River was around 4.30 am. It was clear that they had driven directly from the Nash party in Chatswood to the river—a journey of no more than ten minutes.

Much of the investigation would focus on the party where the victims spent the last hours of their lives.

Surely one of the party guests could cast some light on the puzzling deaths?

Ken and Ruth Nash explained to detectives that every New Year it was customary for them to entertain close friends and the occasional new acquaintance at their home. Strictly invitation only, guests were chosen for their diversity of interests or occupations—surgeons, artists, musicians and scientists, like the talented Dr Bogle.

Short, with a pocked complexion and wiry brown hair, Ken Nash would have looked more at home in a scoutmaster's uniform than a suit and tie. His strikingly attractive wife, Ruth, was every bit the clichéd 'respectable North Shore housewife'. During the Coronial Inquest, reporters would wax lyrical about her looking 'remarkably soignée in her choice of clothes' and her sophisticated repartee. For the party, Ruth had purchased a glamorous, white lamé gown.

'We asked guests to bring a work of art of his or her making', explained Mrs Nash. 'The idea was to create a conversation point to kick-start the evening.'

Gilbert Bogle was the first guest to arrive. His artistic creation was a macabre Picasso-style sketch featuring a two-faced woman with severed limbs. The artworks of other guests varied from the absurd to the humorous, such as a mobile called *Morning*—the component parts of which were an alarm clock, a newspaper and a hard fried egg.[17]

By all accounts, the cheerful, ever garrulous Bogle was the life of the party; flitting between groups and reacquainting himself with those he had met at previous Nash parties. One long-term Nash friend, journalist Leicester Cotton said of Bogle, 'No one who saw him that night could accept the theory that he had the faintest foreknowledge of what was to come.'

At 10.30 that night, Ken Nash had been surprised to find the bearded, bohemian-looking Geoffrey Chandler and his wife Margaret at the door. Nash had entirely forgotten he had invited them ten days earlier after the CSIRO's Murraybank party. According to Leicester Cotton it would have been difficult not to notice their entrance. He described Geoffrey Chandler as a 'tall man, well-built and reminiscent of a buccaneer of (Queen) Elizabeth the first's time with his dark, smouldering red beard and aquiline features. In an otherwise conservatively dressed assembly, he sported a casual short-sleeve shirt, sandals and slacks'.

At first, Margaret Chandler seemed shy, but Cotton believed she appeared bent on enjoying the party. As Ken Nash went for drinks, his wife, Ruth, provided Margaret with a nametag fashioned in the form of an artist's palette.

Bogle wandered over and took over pinning the nametag to her rose-patterned summer dress. She was one of the youngest women in the room—and the prettiest. Geoffrey Chandler overheard the conversation:

'Is your wife here?' Margaret inquired.

'No, our youngest isn't well. I should have stayed at home, I suppose.'

'Yes, I think so.'

'And not see you again?'

Around midnight, Ken Nash became aware of Geoffrey Chandler's absence. He and his wife went out to the front of the house. Chandler's vintage Vauxhall was missing. When they returned inside they noticed Mrs Chandler was also absent. Ken Nash made a further search of the house. He finally found her in the backyard in an embrace with Dr Bogle. Nash told detectives that he turned off the yard light, and they returned to the house immediately. Intriguingly, at the Coronial Inquest, Nash would deny seeing any 'undue friendliness between Dr Bogle and Mrs Chandler'.

On his return to the living room, Dr Bogle selected a record then offered his hand to the hostess and together they entertained the other partygoers with mock Spanish dancing. Bogle then encouraged others to join the dancing with a selection of rock and roll records.

At around 3 am, as supper was served, Ruth Nash noticed Geoffrey Chandler reappear. 'Where had he been for the last three and a half hours?' she thought. Chandler turned down Ken Nash's offer of food and repaired to the bar to pour a gin and bitter lemon for himself and a five-ounce glass of beer for Margaret. After coffee had been served, Ken Nash noticed the Chandlers sitting alone in the study. At about 3.40 am, he noticed Dr Bogle had joined the Chandlers in conversation.

The timing fitted exactly with Chandler's testimony.

At 4.05, according to one guest, Bogle farewelled everybody and departed. A few minutes later, Mrs Nash noticed Margaret standing on the front lawn. When

Margaret realised she had been seen, she glared at Mrs Nash with a 'What are you looking at?' expression, then walked off.

Despite their general appearance of respectability, any one of the guests could have been a possible murderer. Parsons held suspicions about one of the guests, the only single female at the party, a 39-year-old CSIRO research scientist. Detectives discovered that she suffered from depression, possibly due to a chronic skin condition that afflicted her face and arms.

She told Inspector Parsons that Gilbert Bogle worked in the same building. She usually ran into him in the staff tearoom or at a tennis club where they were both members. She said he was a kind man who made a point of kissing her at the party at midnight. By her own admission, she was one of the last people to see him alive. She left the party at the same time as Dr Bogle, at which time he kissed her goodbye. As he drove off in his Ford Prefect, he tooted his horn and waved to her. She told the police she didn't see anyone in the car with him.

Parsons considered the woman a possible suspect. Her colleagues painted a picture of a lonely person who was possibly infatuated with Dr Bogle. Perhaps to alleviate her embarrassment from her skin condition, Bogle regularly made a point of paying her compliments. But she may have mistaken his kindness as a display of affection. When Parsons questioned her about her feelings for Dr Bogle, she became very guarded.

Inquiries with the CSIRO revealed that the woman held a degree in science and that poisons were well within her knowledge. Parsons deduced that she may have indeed seen Mrs Chandler in the car, become jealous, followed them down the lovers' lane and killed them both. But there were problems with this theory. Why would she have had poison in her possession and how did she administer it to two half-naked people so that it could not be identified at autopsy?

Detectives attempted to substantiate the woman's movements after she left the New Year's party. But there was no one to corroborate her arrival home at the beachside suburb of Coogee, thirty minutes later. While she could not be disregarded as a suspect, no evidence linking her to the deaths was forthcoming.

In many ways, the evolving mystery surrounding the deaths bore all the hallmarks of a classic Agatha Christie scenario: a small, cultured group assembled in a refined, colourful setting; someone dies; Detective Hercule Poirot arrives and interviews them all; with few exceptions each guest is a suspect until one by one they are ruled out. In time, using brilliant deductive reasoning, the detective announces a motive, then the method and finally the hapless murderer. But in the Bogle-Chandler case there was little left for Parsons and his team of detectives to deduce.

In the days after the deaths, and before they were questioned, many of the guests had met to discuss the party and make sure their memories aligned. Their statements were thus seriously compromised. Poirot would have fumed.

7. Motive For Murder

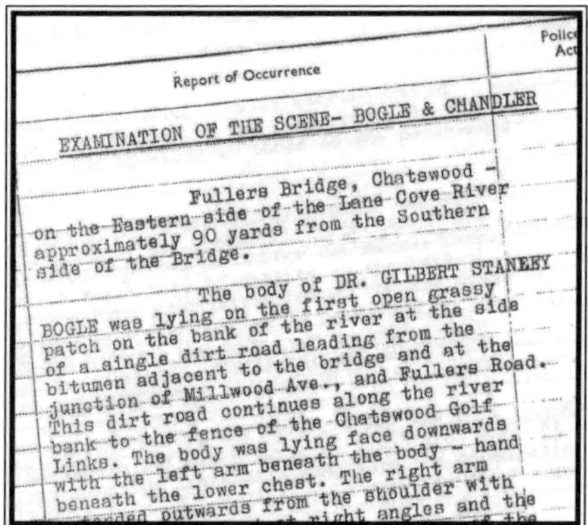

Report of Occurrence

EXAMINATION OF THE SCENE- BOGLE & CHANDLER

Fullers Bridge, Chatswood - on the Eastern side of the Lane Cove River approximately 90 yards from the Southern side of the Bridge.

The body of DR. GILBERT STANLEY BOGLE was lying on the first open grassy patch on the bank of the river at the side of a single dirt road leading from the bitumen adjacent to the bridge and at the junction of Millwood Ave., and Fullers Road. This dirt road continues along the river bank to the fence of the Chatswood Golf Links. The body was lying face downwards with the left arm beneath the body - hand beneath the lower chest. The right arm extended outwards from the shoulder with right angles and the

There can be no easy way to hear of the death of a relative, but the way Geoffrey Chandler's parents, Tom and Hilda, heard of their daughter-in-law's death was cruel and heartless. Holidaying at their Queensland beach house in Coolum, they read of the tragedy the following afternoon in a local newspaper. Tom Chandler immediately telephoned his son's Croydon home, but there was no answer. He then called Margaret's distressed parents.

The following day, Tom and Hilda set off for Sydney, picking up more details of the developing case on the car radio. One news bulletin reported that their son, Geoffrey, had gone into hiding. On the morning of 5 January, they drove into western Sydney. As they approached the Morphett home in Granville, they noticed a newspaper banner declaring 'Murder Most Likely'.

Fearing the couple would be caught up in the publicity, the Morphetts had arranged accommodation for them at a Burwood motel under the assumed name of Schafer. The following day, Geoffrey Chandler arrived at their motel room. On seeing his mother, he broke down and was inconsolable:

> I had overwhelming grief and shock. Part of grief is the sort of thing...why? Then you've got the question, what if? The 'what ifs' and 'why' and so forth are the guilt. After all, I could have said to Margaret, okay, no deal, you're coming with me. But I was selfish and was excited by the thrill of charging through the night to sort of forbidden fruits. Who wouldn't be, I guess.

Geoffrey was Tom and Hilda's only child, born in Stanthorpe, southeast Queensland on 5 May 1930. Tom Chandler was a community-minded country schoolteacher. Hilda was nine years younger—an age disparity not uncommon in those sparsely populated parts. During Tom's early career, the family moved around the state from school to school.

By the time Geoffrey started his senior education, he had already attended five schools, including Darnley Island, a volcanic outcrop situated in the eastern section of the Torres Strait, which was home to a few hundred Indigenous people.

As soon as Geoffrey settled into one place, his

father would announce yet another transfer. It was a healthy, vagabond existence, but having to continually walk away from friendships was difficult. Over time, Geoffrey found it simpler to be self-sufficient.

High school was more settled. Tom took a posting at Glen View State School in the Mooloolah River Valley. Geoffrey attended nearby Nambour High School where he would do well in both his junior and senior examinations. He grew tall and willowy, with carrot-red hair. On one hand, he was slightly introverted and quiet in company. On the other, he drew attention to himself with his obsessions. Bright and practical, he tinkered in his spare time with all things mechanical, particularly automobiles. It was wartime and the number of broken down cars in small towns was understandably proportional to the number of mechanics seconded to the battlefront. In 1950, he moved to Sydney where he secured a job with Australia's premier electronics manufacturer, AWA, first as a process worker, then as a cadet engineer.

His skills were in demand, gaining him employment with a number of electronics firms, before he moved onto the government scientific organisation, CSIRO. There, he worked on the creation of one of the world's first computers and the early development of radar for aeronautics.

The Chandlers knew little about their son's life in Sydney. He'd arrived a 20-year-old virgin and quickly gravitated toward a social group called 'the Push' where a sexual revolution was underway. Influenced by Scottish-born Challis Professor of Philosophy at Sydney

University, John Anderson, as well as the Libertarians and the Free-thinker's Society, Push members were generally anti-moralist, anti-authoritarian and supporters of sexual freedom, who also liked to drink a great deal.

CONTENTS OF LADIES HANDBAG IN SUITCASE TAKEN POSSESSION

OF FROM 17 CROMWELL STREET, CROYDON.

1 front door key, No. 17 Cromwell Street, Croydon.
1 "Relide" ladies wrist watch with broken band.
1 Envelope addressed, "Mrs. G.A. Chandler, 17 Cromwell St
Croydon," and posted from Eudlo, Queensland, the back
which had been used as a shopping list.
1 Card - Dr. Ian A. McDonald, 182 Collins Street, Melbou
1 Driver's License in name of Mrs. Margaret Olive Chandle
1 Commonwealth Savings Bank book cover.
1 Baby Health Centre card.

Entertainer Barry Humphries colourfully described the Push as 'a fraternity of middle-class desperates, journalists, drop-out academics, gamblers and poets manqués, and their doxies'.[18] Humphries himself was a member, along with other soon-to-be influential people of the arts and publishing world, including writer Bob Ellis, artist John Olsen, filmmaker Margaret Fink, publisher Richard Neville and feminist-author Germaine Greer.

> Here are these highly exciting, interesting, exhilarating people who made quite good intellectual contributions to the philosophy of life in those days. It was a good period and I was caught up in all of this.

By his own admission, Chandler was not of the Push's high-profile centre. He orbited the fringe, but was still able to indulge in its various vices:

> The fundamental concept in libertarianism and Anderson's philosophy was 'freedom'. So instead of being constrained by conventional morality, conventional religion and conventional society, you had freedom to indulge whatever you liked, if you wanted to drink or whatever. Sex didn't have barriers. The concept of it was that if you wanted to have sex with somebody who was mutually attractive then fine, you went and did it. You didn't have to wait to go and get married or become engaged with someone. And I was the innocent who stumbled across this honey pot, so to speak.

While covering the case, *Bulletin* journalist Peter Kelly painted the Push through seemingly conservative eyes:

> Their chief claim to notoriety, in most of the public's eyes, lies in their belief in 'free love' or what some 1920s Americans (from whom many of their ideas derive) call 'trial marriage'. In conversation, the *Lady Chatterley* four-letter word is probably the most used swear word or term of endearment—both sexes use it as freely as most Australians use 'bloody'.

Even after marrying Margaret, Geoffrey Chandler continued to indulge in Push activities. Dozens of his Push associates attended the couple's housewarming party at their Croydon home. Margaret was not a member, but she apparently grew to tolerate Geoffrey's eccentric friends with their unconventional view of the world.

The Balmain New Year's party, which Geoffrey escaped to, was an annual Push affair, hosted by left-wing economist Ken Buckley. According to Anne Coombs, author of *Sex and Anarchy*, it was one of the best Push parties ever:

> It had an extraordinary atmosphere. People were wandering in and out all night. It was a rambling house, set in a large garden. There was space for amorous encounters in the dimly lit rooms. Some people recall seeing Chandler there, out in the backyard or having a drink on the other side of a room, but no one had taken much notice.

Following the deaths of his wife and Dr Bogle, Geoffrey Chandler anticipated that his Push associates would suffer because of their association with him. Indeed, once word got out of Chandler's Push connection, reporters and photographers headed to its headquarters—the Royal George Hotel, beside Sydney's busy dock area.

A *Daily Telegraph* headline blared: 'The Beatniks Go For Cover'. Despite offers of free beer and money, the 'beatniks' and 'bohemians' drew a curtain of silence against outsiders. Many stopped frequenting the hotel until the case died down.

The *Daily Mirror*'s new feature writer, Gerald Stone, fresh from the *New York Times*, was given the task of tracking down the elusive Geoffrey Chandler:

> They said, 'We want you to go to the Royal George Hotel.' Now this is the place where The Push bohemian life of Sydney revolved around. They wanted me to find this

> Chandler fellow who sported a beard. So I was off the boat walking into this pub and finding everybody had a beard! Even the women seemed to have beards! So it was a very funny experience.[19]

Geoffrey Chandler did all he could to keep his face out of the newspapers:

> If I didn't want a picture, then that should have been it. But these vultures just persisted and persisted and persisted, and went to extraordinary lengths to try and get pictures. I went to extraordinary lengths to stay away from them, to avoid being seen. It's my privacy and they should respect it, and they just absolutely didn't. And the more they didn't, the more I refused to cooperate with them.

When a press photographer staked out Chandler's laboratory at Sydney University, the camera-shy Chandler escaped detection by leaving work every day via the back entrance and lying down in the rear seat of a colleague's car. In the end, the photographer worked out what was happening and captured the back of Chandler's head while seated in the rear of a taxi. That photograph made the front page and painted an image of a man on the run.

After a tip off, Chandler was again snapped in the beer garden of a Camperdown hotel in the company of an unidentified blonde woman. Wearing short sleeves and rolled-up slacks, Chandler looked pensive. The unidentified woman was his lover, Pam Logan.

Detectives were still looking into Logan's background. A female friend of both Chandler and Logan told police that they had been seeing each other longer than Chandler had admitted. Moreover, Logan had fallen pregnant. Sniffing a possible motive for murder, detectives discovered Logan's name in the records of King George V Hospital for Mothers and Babies.

In May 1962, seven months before the deaths, Logan fronted up to hospital admission claiming she had just miscarried and required a curette. A medical examination revealed that the pregnancy was still viable and she was sent on her way.

Detectives interviewed a hospital social worker. She recalled that a man accompanied Logan to the hospital, a man who had acted in the role of 'adviser'. From a photograph, the social worker identified the man as Geoffrey Chandler.

Detectives drove to a terrace in nearby Annandale where Logan was now in hiding from the press, and put her through another harrowing interrogation about two dead people whom she claimed she had never met.

They asked whether Chandler had ever discussed the possibility of divorcing his wife. She denied that any such discussion had taken place. They had an understanding, she said, that if either wanted to end it then that was too bad for the other. They asked if she had fallen pregnant to Chandler, to which she replied, 'Definitely not. I know how to look after myself. I'm not a child.'

Under pressure, Logan did confess to having falling pregnant to Chandler but refused to say what happened to the child.

Every lie or obfuscation on Logan's part seemed to weaken the strength of Chandler's alibi. Was Logan telling the truth about being with Chandler at the time his wife was at the river? Or had he forced her to lie to protect him?

Fortunately for both Chandler and Logan, three independent witnesses had contacted the police to say they had seen Chandler in his distinctive vintage car at exactly the times and places he had claimed to be at various locations on New Year's morning. One witness had seen Chandler driving to the other side of the city through the Harbour Bridge tollgates at 4.15 am—around the time Dr Bogle and Mrs Chandler were driving to the Lane Cove River. Therefore, Geoffrey Chandler could not have been at the river at the time of the deaths.

◆ ◆ ◆

Geoffrey Chandler's parents knew nothing of his double-life in Sydney and he wanted to keep it that way. They desperately wanted an explanation for what had happened to his wife, but he insisted he couldn't provide it. He swore he had no idea why Margaret was dead.

He told them he was relying on friends to put him up, moving every few days to keep the press off his tail. Margaret's family was caring for the boys and the whole tragedy was a nightmare for everyone concerned. There was nothing his parents could do but to go home and stay out of it. Reluctantly, Tom and Hilda took his advice and left Sydney the following day. Meanwhile, their only son went back into hiding.

Register No. 131/2 16th May, 1963.

Death of Margaret Olive Chandler
and Gilbert Stanley Bogle

I, Vivian Claude Mahoney, hereby certify as follows:

(1) My scientific qualifications are:

Bachelor of Science of the University of Queensland;
Associate of the Royal Australian Chemical Institute;
Associate of the Royal Institute of Chemistry.

(2) On 3rd January, 1963, Mr. E. S. Ogg, Government Analyst handed to me the following exhibits for examination:

1. Bottle labelled "Ekatin" taken from 12 Waratah Street, Chatswood.
2. Bottle labelled "Flurets" containing 25 tablets.
3. Bottle labelled "Simpson's Pharmacy" containing quantity of green tablets.
4. Bottle labelled "New Gammawash".
5. Bottle labelled "Ascorbic Acid" containing one tablet.
6. Bottle labelled "Paxy Cream."
7. Unlabelled bottle containing four white tablets.
8. Bottle labelled "Vasylox".
9. Unlabelled carton containing ten capsules.
10. Bottle labelled "Abdec Drops".
11. Bottle labelled "Corio" whisky.
12. Bottle labelled "Cornwell's" vinegar.
13. Bottle labelled "Cawarra Claret".
14. Bottle labelled "White Horse" whisky.
15. Bottle labelled "Murlex".

8. Poison

A double murderer was on the loose and he or she could strike again; that was the bottom line for the NSW Police. They had a formidable track record for hunting down killers. In the previous year, 1962, they had solved all but one of the fifty-two homicides in the State and all the culprits were behind bars. But there was something strikingly different about the Bogle-Chandler case; there was no obvious cause of death. Solving the mystery would have to depend not so much on 'old school' detective work but science.

'Forensics' was not a term widely used in early 1960s Sydney policing. Few detectives availed themselves of university or college courses in forensic science.

Former chief of the Scientific Branch, Norm Merchant:

> If we wanted to know about ballistics, we shot bullets into all types of materials and studied the results. I learned first hand about the dangers of such experiments when a bullet ricocheted off a hard surface and went right through my leg.[20]

Tall and quietly spoken, Sergeant George Lindsay gravitated to the job because he knew about photographic chemicals. His knowledge came from books and experience gained on the ground:

> We would take full control of the scene, produce photographs of the bodies then photograph every part of the area. We drew plans of the location for the Court. And later we had to deal with professors and experts in all different fields. This allowed the local police to go and knock on doors and ask questions.[21]

On New Year's Day, Lindsay searched the riverside track and muddy riverbed with his more senior colleague, Allen Clarke. Pallid-faced with slicked down hair, the unassuming Clarke was at the top of his craft. Three years earlier, he had worked on the headline-grabbing Graeme Thorne kidnapping/murder case. The schoolboy's decomposing body, wrapped in a rug, had been dumped in a scrub-covered vacant lot at Seaforth, north of Sydney. From the detritus found on the rug, Clarke helped detectives construct a picture of where he believed the boy had been killed by strangulation: a brick house with pink mortar, with two varieties of cypress trees in the garden and a dog, possibly a Pekinese. From these clues the home was identified and the killer was brought to justice.

But for Clarke and Lindsay, the Bogle Chandler 'crime scene' offered no hard evidence. On the mudflats below Dr Bogle's body, they found a couple of used condoms, but these seemed too old. An envelope, containing a letter, was discovered nearby, but it proved to have no connection with either victim. A few containers were found and analysed but did not contain toxic chemicals. The most important discovery was of two indentations on the mudflats, which matched Margaret Chandler's knees and traces of a lace pattern similar to that of her slip. Faeces below the bank led Clarke to believe that Bogle too had been on the riverbed. From Dr Bogle's clothing, they took sweepings from both trouser and coat pockets, but like those from Bogle's car they revealed nothing remotely useful to their inquiry. Clarke and Lindsay went to the Nash home in Chatswood, collecting leftover food from the garbage bin, including pieces of chicken, radish, lettuce, celery, ham, sausage, tomato and cheese.

The Nash home

A most surprising discovery was the minimal amount of alcohol consumed. But this matched the guests' description of a sober party. Moreover, no alcohol would be found in the blood specimens of either victim.

At the Chandlers' Croydon home, they gathered medicines and household chemicals, including weed killer. The following morning, at Pamela Logan's Darlington terrace, they took possession of a jar of peanut butter, a bottle of Meta-Kleen and a tin of Fissolve and delivered them to the Government Analyst to be tested against the victims' tissue samples.

Toxicologist Vivian Mahoney had set up two separate methods in which common drugs and poisons could be easily identified:

> Poisons have either got to be organic or inorganic. In the normal analytical procedures strychnine, arsenic, cyanide, pesticides, agricultural poisons, barbiturates and sleeping tablets, even things like rat poisons, all those are very easily picked up within the first day or two. If you didn't come up with an answer in about three days you would immediately realise that there's something unusual or something that was slipping through the net—and there weren't too many of those.

A poison is defined as a substance that can injure the health of a living organism or destroy life outright. In a broader context, poisons include prescription drugs, designed to benefit a person, and illicit drugs—it all comes down to dosage. The police running sheet would soon list hundreds of possible poisons; beryllium, barium carbonate, croton oil, malathion, sleeping tablets, cobalt, parathion, barbital, phenobarb and dieldrin. The suggested methods of delivery of poisons were exotic and bizarre: lipstick, hypodermic needles and brown jumper ants. The most difficult problem is to connect a possible poison to a manner of delivery and then to reason why it occurred: murder; murder/suicide; double/suicide; accidental death or even a practical joke that went wrong.

If it were an accident, toxicologists would first consider contaminated food or drink. Food-borne botulism was high on Mahoney's list. One millionth of a gram of botulinum toxin is lethal in humans, but only a handful of cases occur in Australia each year. There were obvious problems with the botulism theory; symptoms normally take twelve to thirty-six hours to appear. Only in rare cases can death occur within six hours. Dinner was not served at the Nash party until after 2.30 am and Bogle and Chandler were most certainly dead or dying around 5 am. More importantly, no one else at the party was ill.

During the party, one of the guests, Jack Booty-Johnson, had several conversations with Dr Bogle, and was with him during supper. After consuming the hot food from his own plate, Johnson told police he had 'consumed a portion of the food on the Doctor's plate'. He added the handshake Bogle gave him as he left the party was very firm and he seemed to be in the normal 'Gib Bogle state of mind—calm, happy and well'.

Statistically, poisoning accounts for less than 2 per cent of all murders in Australia. Most poisoners use something common and easily available. In 1950s

Australia, the most popular poison was thallium, the main ingredient in rat and ant poisons. More toxic than mercury and lead, thallium is odourless and tasteless, and therefore easily added to food or put in a drink. The most famous thallium poisoner was 63-year-old Caroline Grills, dubbed 'Aunt Thally'. Grills was arrested in 1953 and charged with killing four members of her family after adding the poison to tea, biscuits and cakes. After a spate of fifty other cases, thallium was placed on the banned poisons list.

A decade later, detectives investigating the Bogle-Chandler deaths believed that only a very determined, highly educated murderer, such as a professional chemist, doctor or toxicologist could get away undetected with a double poisoning. From the beginning they believed Geoffrey Chandler might be such a person.

'Do you have a knowledge of poisons?' Parsons asked Chandler.

'Elementary knowledge acquired during the course of university education.'

'In respect to what particular poisons?'

'Strychnine, arsenic, weed killer. My knowledge of these poisons is confined to knowing that these substances are poisonous and that a certain amount of knowledge is required to administer them.'

'Do you have that knowledge?'

'Not really, no.'

'Have you any knowledge as to how the particular poisons that you mention affect the human being?'

'I know that they all produce stomach cramps, and

that the effects are unpleasant. I want to mention at this point that I find the taking of human life completely beyond me.'

The poker-faced Chandler had an alibi. He was nowhere near the Lane Cove River when the couple were dying. But if he had poisoned the couple at the party, then his alibi counted for little.

After three days of analysis, however, Mahoney had detected no poison in either victim's tissue samples:

> It was obvious that what killed one killed the other but nothing was coming out. Everything was coming up negative. They both had a little bit of caffeine and that's all.

The mystery was deepening and now the victims, Dr Bogle and Mrs Chandler, seemed to be conspiring with their killer.

9. Bitter Pill

Mrs Sheridan Pausey

On 2 January 1963, Mrs Sheridan Pausey got the shock of her life:

It was a very hot day and I decided to take a break. I turned on the television and lay down on the sofa. A photograph came on the screen and I looked at it and I couldn't believe it. I called out to my husband, 'Steve that's Margaret. She's dead.' And he said, 'Who?' and I said, 'Margaret Chandler. It turns out she is dead. Murdered!'[22]

A celebrity in dog-breeding circles, Sheridan Pausey ran Windswept Kennels. Margaret's first dog, a dachshund called Biddy, was crossed with Mrs Pausey's prize-winning dachshund, Windswept Climax.

A few days after the news broke Mrs Pausey was startled to find the police at her front door. While sifting through the Chandler home for evidence, they had discovered a brown handbag. Inside, they found a receipt from Windswept Kennels.

> I got a bit of shock because two detectives were standing there asking me my name. I asked them in and they asked if Margaret Chandler had visited me. Well I said, 'Yes. She brought her puppies out for me to look at and give an opinion and she stayed talking, chatting. I even remember she was wearing a pale blue floral dress. It was a very hot afternoon and we had some lemonade, I think.' They asked if I knew Geoff Chandler. I said, 'Yes, I'd met him.' They asked me if I knew how the Chandlers got along and I said, 'Well, I've seen them together. They seemed like a perfectly normal married couple and I had met them through the dogs and we'd had quite a few meetings and I met the children.' As I say the word normal came to mind. And they said, 'What time did she leave?' and I said, 'Well she left about five, and I had the impression she was going out that evening.' Well the police were a mixed bunch. There was a young fellow who was obviously sympathetic towards him. But I got the impression that some of them were not. One of them said they were after him. It almost seemed as if he was being hunted!

The detectives questioned Mrs Pausey about Mrs Chandler's mood on the day she visited. She said that Margaret had given the impression that something was worrying her and she appeared depressed. She also noticed that Margaret was not as particular about her appearance, as she had been previously:

> Margaret was quite a nice-looking girl. Fairly sturdy, brown hair and very fresh complexion; the type of woman that you'd say would be wholesome. We started talking as women do. It turned out she had had a disagreement with her husband and I remember saying, 'Oh they should burn all men', which made her laugh. Geoffrey? Well the first words that come to mind, which is strange for a man, is rather gentle. He was a tall man but he had a very soft voice, a well-spoken voice. He didn't impress me as a man with a terribly strong character but at the same time, he struck me as a man who would have quite a brilliant mind but not a man who would talk too much about it—a typical scientist. He spoke to Margaret and the children and the dogs in a gentle manner. When I say gentle, I mean kind and soft. He had this beard and I think that this was the attraction to the newspapers. They didn't often get a young man with a beard but he was always extremely polite to me. They bred as a hobby and they were very fond of the dogs. I never saw him do the wrong thing by his wife or his children or his dogs.

The detectives then showed Mrs Pausey the receipt they'd found and asked whether she had given Mrs Chandler some pills:

> I told them, 'Yes, I had given her some pills for tapeworm—Hydarex.' They were very newly on the market, only possibly a few vets and a few breeders had them at that point in time. They asked me if they were safe. Well they were marked dangerous and not sold for human consumption so I said, 'No they're not safe for people to sit and guzzle.' But thinking of the children I had told her this. She had been a nurse I felt she was responsible, I mean, there would be some people I wouldn't give them to.

It was the first real lead and was immediately leaked to the media:

> The press at this point in time were pretty desperate for anything. The fact that I'd given her some pills of course was meat and drink to the newspapers. There was a full-page poster with the headline, 'She Sold The Pills' with my name on it. It was dreadfully embarrassing because it made me look as if perhaps I might have done the deed. And all I had done was give her some worm pills!

A reporter went to the Chandler home and found their dogs, seemingly abandoned. Tabloid creativity then reached another milestone when a press photographer placed the puppies in socks and pegged them onto the Chandler clothesline. Soon after, Mrs Pausey received a phone call from Geoffrey Chandler's solicitor:

> It seems that the RSPCA had taken his dogs and frankly I think it might have been to put some pressure on him

> because I couldn't think of why the dogs would be taken away from him. And the solicitor said, 'Would I look after the dogs for him?' and I said, 'Well, yes I would.' Well, the press was so desperate they were even out there with cameras to photograph me taking the dogs! Mr Chandler subsequently rang me two or three times to see about the welfare of the dogs and I said, 'Yes, they're coming on very well.' And I think I kept them until after the Inquest. I was pleased to do a kind deed but it was all such a complete and utter jamboree for the newspapers.

Daily Mirror reporter Bill Jenkings would go to his grave believing that the worming tablets had killed the couple. He argued that someone—most likely Geoffrey Chandler—had spiked their drinks with the tablets as a practical joke to spoil their romantic tryst, but he gave them too high a dose and it proved fatal.

Jenkings' practical joke theory falls down on one basic fact: Hydarex, which vets had used to purge worms from a dog's intestine since 1921, is extremely bitter tasting. It requires the addition of 10 times an amount of sucrose to Hydarex to mask its foul taste. If it were a practical joke, Geoffrey Chandler would have had to know about its bitter taste, had access to sucrose and negotiated the sweetening of two drinks without witnesses. Moreover, if sucrose had not been added, Dr Bogle and Mrs Chandler would certainly have noticed the sour taste and discontinued drinking.

Under police questioning, Geoffrey Chandler denied any knowledge of the worming tablets. A further search of the Chandler house failed to uncover the tablets. Scientific detectives delivered a quantity of Hydarex worming tablets to the Government Analyst for testing.

Toxicologist Viv Mahoney believed the dog worming theory was flawed from the start:

> Every label has on it 'poisonous'. But if you look at the toxicity of those [Hydarex] tablets; they're not poisonous. Considerable quantities would have to be consumed before they killed you.[23]

After being hounded by the newspapers, Mrs Pausey was relieved to hear chemical analysis of the victims' tissues proved negative:

> They had run routine tests and nothing had turned up for which I was eternally grateful. They ran so many tests and they just didn't seem to be able to come up with what exactly killed them.

Mrs Pausey did see Geoffrey Chandler again. Her instincts told her that he was not the 'killer type':

> Geoffrey came up to say thank you once to our house and we sat and talked about things. He looked very, very tired. He'd had a dreadful time. I asked after the children. He said they were fine. He seemed concerned about them all. I know that he was having a very bad time because the newspapers were chasing him from one place to the other.

Mrs Sheridan Pausey, like the public at large, had heard rumours going around about the Chandlers:

> I know there was all sorts of talk about them being a swinging couple. At that stage there was one club I belonged to, which did have a lot of swinging couples, but they were quite different than the Chandlers. Who knows with Margaret, but I can't imagine it. She might have been done up in her best and this man might have charmed the birds off the trees, but I wouldn't see her as being terribly open with her favours. Perhaps this was the one time she did fall. Even so, sex doesn't kill you.

Mrs Chandler and her dachshunds

10. Tabloid War

"WEIRD CULTS" TIP IN DEATHS PUZZLE

As each day passed, pressure increased on both the police and the Government Analyst to come up with a solution to the growing Bogle Chandler mystery. The bulk of the pressure came from the media.

The story happened to break at a time when Sydney was in the midst of a vicious war between two tabloid afternoon newspapers, the *Sun* and the *Daily Mirror*. That war would not only have a profound effect on public opinion, but also on the running of the investigation. Freshly imported from the *New York Times*, Gerald Stone was the *Mirror*'s new feature writer:

> Their life-blood was to come up with stories that could win. They were like two professional wrestlers trying to appeal to the readers. By any standard, the Bogle-Chandler case was a sensational crime story; apparent

> lovers in an adulterous relationship, ending up semi-naked and dead on the bank of a river. And so it was all stops out to try to come up with the angle of what happened? Why were these people dead? It wasn't as if somebody had been shot and stabbed or something like that. So these two newspapers were at each other's throats for the biggest headlines.

In the early 1960s, newspaper police roundsmen seemed to have a symbiotic, usually alcohol-fuelled, relationship with certain Criminal Investigation Branch detectives. Veteran *Mirror* crime reporter Bill Jenkings' preferred 'office' was a hotel near CIB headquarters in central Sydney. On New Year's morning, Jenkings was clocking in at the bar of the Century Hotel when the publican's phone rang. It was the Reception Officer at the CIB. A body had been found beside the Lane Cove River. Jenkings was off in a flash and filed a front-page story for the afternoon edition. His competition at the *Sun*, Noel Bailey, was out of contact and missed the breaking story entirely.[24]

The *Mirror* had won the first salvo, but the following day it was game on.

On 2 January, before the results of the autopsy were known, both the *Mirror* and the *Sun* reported that the Government Psychiatrist, Dr John McGeorge, had postulated: 'The couple could have gone through a strange sort of death ritual. There may have been some deep emotional entanglement.'

It was a ludicrous claim; Bogle and Chandler had only met once prior to their deaths.

Over night, both tabloids tracked down a picture of Bogle for the front page. Obtaining a photograph of Mrs Chandler was not so simple, as Gerald Stone recalled:

> The Holy Grail in this story was to find a photo of Margaret Chandler. There had been photos published of Bogle and the Nashes and this type of thing but nobody really knew what Margaret Chandler looked like—this mystery nurse. So my first job was to go around trying to track down a photo.

The following day, 3 January, the *Mirror* claimed another victory in the tabloid war with a full front-page photograph of Margaret Chandler taken on her nursing graduation day:

> Each afternoon the paper had this shouting poster, and of course they did anything they could to hype it up. They used to say, 'Exclusive', that was one thing. But 'First Photo' that was a major thing.

When the post-mortem examination of the bodies proved inconclusive an unnamed reporter on the *Mirror* confidently claimed:

> The couple were killed by strychnine. It was taken in capsules ... It is believed Mrs Chandler may have tried to drag herself down to the riverbank to quench a thirst induced by strychnine.

There was no evidence to back this theory at all. In

fact, strychnine was one of the first poisons tested for and it came up negative.

At his Chatswood home, party host Ken Nash happily allowed photographers to tramp from room to room—even before scientific detectives had scoured it for evidence. Meanwhile, the *Mirror*'s Bill Jenkings hovered between the City Morgue and the Government Analyst building trying to extract any titbit, which would make a good story:

> I knew this story was fast becoming one of the biggest with which any of us reporters had ever been involved.

LATE FINAL EXTRA

THE SUN

"ABOVE ALL" "FOR AUSTRALIA"

16,502. THURSDAY, JANUARY 17, 1963.

E

Ask for HUTTON'S A&R SALAMI

Lotteries: No. 5086, P. 50; No. 5087, P. 56. • TV, P. 54. • Finance, P. 42. • City forecast: Further rain; N-E winds

CREAM WITH BRIGHT RED ROSES

DEATH DRESS OF MRS CHANDLER

Mrs Margaret Chandler died on the bank of the Lane Cove River early on New Year's Day wearing a cream ballerina party frock with a printed motif of bright red roses.

This was revealed today when the police allowed Pressmen to photograph the colourful death dress at C.I.B. headquarters.

Yesterday the police disclosed for the first time that a piece of old brownish carpet had been spread over the body of Dr Gilbert Bogle as he lay 17 yards from Mrs Chandler on the river bank.

APPEAL TO PUBLIC

C.I.B. chief, Det.-Supt. R. J. Walden, today appealed to members of the public to study photographs of the carpet and the dress in the hope that:

- Someone may be able to say who owned the piece of carpet and when it was tossed away at the death scene;
- Someone may have seen Mrs Chandler between the time she left the New Year's Eve party at Chatswood at 4.30 a.m. on January 1 and the time her body was found approximately four hours later.

Mrs Chandler's frock has narrow shoulder straps, flared skirt and the roses are buds and full blooms intermingled with vivid green leaves.

THIRD PERSON THEORY, P. 3

Millions were sold on the back of this mystery story. The nation lapped up every word.

Sydney's broadsheet, the *Sydney Morning Herald*, avoided too much speculation and tried to keep to the facts. As luck would have it, one of the *Herald*'s journalists, Leicester Cotton, was a guest at the Nash party. While Cotton and his wife were amongst the first to leave the party, they were able to provide valuable inside information about the other guests and arrange for interviews with those willing to talk.

By the end of the first week, however, the story threatened to run out of steam.

'Two Deaths Enquiry Dead End', claimed the *Mirror*. The Government Analyst, Mr Ogg, told the newspaper that his staff had worked through the weekend but there was still no breakthrough. The fact that the toxicologists still could not determine what killed the couple was both a story and a blow for future circulation.

The police told reporters that the case might not be solved. Airing their frustration through the media seemed to be designed to pressure the toxicologists. The dignified Ogg proclaimed his department would 'not sacrifice efficiency for speed'.

The same day, the police delivered to the Government Analyst a parcel of twenty chemicals and drugs taken from the Chandler home including: Fluret tablets, ascorbic acid, weed killer and two bottles of whisky. These joined dozens of other items taken from the Bogle home and food and drinks served at the Nash party. Each item would have to be tested against the tissue samples.

But every specific test required the destruction of a quantity of an organ and Vivian Mahoney feared he might run out of tissue samples before the actual poison was detected:

> From all around Australia and all around the world, suggestions were flooding in and landing on my desk. Some of them I'd already looked at and some of them were so way out that it was wasting my time looking. Some of these rare things that were coming in like Amazon poison darts used in the jungle to kill animals. It was always pretty fanciful to me, but I had to go ahead and look for it. I'd get a letter from a Minister down through the Director of Health, down through my boss to say, 'Analyse it for this because somebody overseas thinks it could be that.' You got to do it but you use up a lot of sample unfortunately. Let's face it, there's only a limit to the amount of stomach, liver, kidney, spleen, intestine. I put to Mr Ogg that if I was going to go through all these way out requests, I was going to eventually run out of sample.

With no new leads in the case, the *Mirror* editor pressed feature writer Gerald Stone to find a new angle. Nine days after the deaths, he conjured up a theory peppered with Cold War spice:

> Of course, a story like this attracts a lot of rumour mongering and when you don't know you kind of make it up. So it was natural that you said, well what else could this guy be doing that everybody's suspicious of? And in

> those days, which was the height of the Cold War and everyone worried about the atomic bomb, stories about a death ray or a secret nuclear thing or working for the CIA, were grist for the mill. So until the Inquest started the press was wide open in its speculation.

Stone wrote that Dr Bogle was a world expert in masers and rumour had it that his work had defence implications. The readership of the *Mirror* was led to believe that masers equated to Ray Guns. Japanese Godzilla films of the 1930s had featured so-called maser weapons, which fired intense electric beams, like amplified microwaves.

How or why Bogle could become a victim of his own creation in a lovers' lane was never fully explained. Besides, in the 1960's, masers were far from portable. Photos of Bogle's laboratory reveal that his research maser filled an entire room.

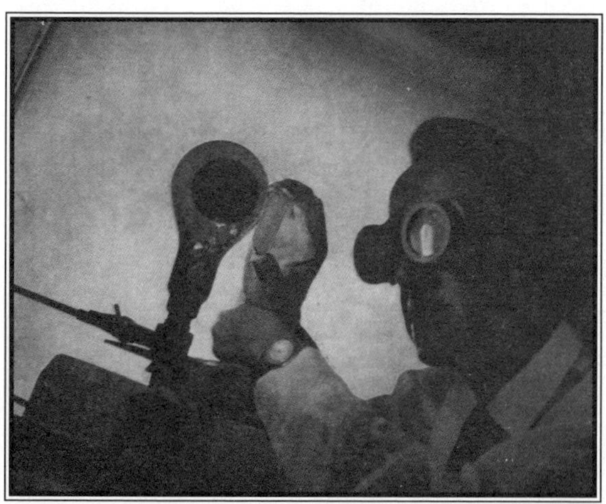

Dr Bogle's death ray

More to the point, the applications for Bogle's Rubidium Maser were primarily astronomy and communications, not for fighting giant lizards like Godzilla or communist invaders.

In April 1961, Bogle penned a tongue-in-cheek article about how masers work for the *Australian Scientist* magazine, subtitled, 'Death Ray, My Eye':

> It has been suggested in the press that the optical maser is a potential death ray, but I believe it would be dangerous only to the eye. Even if the present optical maser operated continuously the power wattage would be only about 100 watts. At a distance of 600 feet the beam would spread to cover a circle a foot diameter and the strength of the illumination would be only about the same as that of sunshine...The enemy need only use goggles and white ointment. Far more power would be needed before this kind of death ray could do any large-scale damage.

But Gerald Stone's story sold newspapers and like many other flights of journalistic imagination, it manipulated the direction of the investigation.

CIB detectives contacted Alfred Harvey, the Senior Principal Research Officer at the CSIRO's Department of Physics, to see if Bogle's work could have had something to do with his death. Harvey told them that Dr Bogle was not engaged in any research that might be called a 'death ray' and he was not involved in research into anything that might have international repercussions on grounds of security. The police ultimately added 'death rays' to their growing list of improbable theories, but in the absence of any other viable answer, many normal, rational people began to believe that sinister Cold War forces were responsible for the deaths.

On the tenth day of the investigation, with still no breakthrough, the State Opposition leader, Bob Askin, demanded the Government post a reward of £5000—a sizable amount, which could have purchased a brand-new home.

Not only had the Bogle-Chandler case become a political issue, it was about to take on the complexion of a television game show with respectable scientists contesting the prize.

Sydney University pharmacologist Professor Roland Thorp offered the services of his laboratory 'to aid in the search of the mystery poison'. The State Government pressured the police to accept the offer, who inturn pressured the Government Analyst, Mr Ogg. Toxicologist Vivian Mahoney was forced to divide up his precious tissue stomach samples and deliver them to Professor Thorp's lab. When Mahoney arrived at the university to hand over the samples, Thorp ushered him to the rear of the building where press photographers were waiting. With a 'thumbs up', Thorp had got much needed publicity for his laboratory and simultaneously humiliated Mahoney and Ogg by suggesting their facilities were inadequate for tracing the poison.

Thorp's laboratory specialised in cardiac pharmacology. Using intestinal strips of a rabbit and a guinea pig, and later chicken and cat hearts, his research assistants conducted experiments to determine the presence of a cardiac poison.

Vivian Mahoney saw Professor Thorp as a publicity seeker, who hoped the high profile case would attract fresh funding for his laboratory. But Thorp was not the only scientist attracting media attention. Government Psychiatrist, Dr John McGeorge, grabbed headlines yet again when he suggested the killer was far smarter than the police or the scientists involved.

'There are poisons that cannot be detected', he said. 'The Bogle-Chandler killer would be congratulating himself that he was getting away with it.'

McGeorge said he had interviewed more than five hundred murderers and believed a confession should not be expected: 'Killers, especially poisoners who must plan their murder, aren't bothered by their consciences.'

Two weeks into the case, the cosy relationship between the CIB and the press came back to haunt the police. The much-publicised 'lack of a breakthrough' forced the Police Commissioner, Norman Allan, to take charge of the investigation. Allan, who had been Commissioner for less than a year, was an enigma to his fellow police. On the one hand he could be charming, persuasive and compassionate, on the other, autocratic and ruthless.[25] The Commissioner came to the case refreshed. In fact, he had been on holidays during the first weeks of the investigation and had simply followed the unfolding Bogle-Chandler case in the newspapers. His strategy was to keep the press on side, by leaking any new piece of information. Insiders believed Allan hoped to take the glory when the mystery was ultimately solved. To the chagrin of the detectives working night and day on the case, Commissioner Allan called in his 'top investigator', Detective Sergeant Jack Bateman, 'to restart the inquiry'.

A key player in the recent Graeme Thorne kidnap/murder case, the press dubbed Bateman 'Father Confessor' when the killer admitted his crime. For his investigation of the Bogle-Chandler case, Bateman told a *Mirror* reporter that he would take a psychological approach in reinterviewing the party guests.

But by now the newspapers wanted less Freud and more results. Frustration reached its high point on 19 January when investigators finally announced the source of the carpet found draped over Dr Bogle's back. Under the cynical banner headline, 'Sherlocks', a *Mirror* editorial quipped:

> After an 18-day investigation police have established the carpet, which covered Dr Gilbert Bogle, came from his own car. We applaud this fine piece of detection.

On Day 20, a front-page headline in the self-proclaimed 'clean family newspaper', the *Sunday Telegraph*, boasted, 'Weird Cults Tip in Deaths Puzzle'. The paper suggested that detectives were investigating a lead that the couple were involved in 'Weird rites, including Black Masses'. A black mass, the story explained, 'is a blasphemous parody of a religious service involving sexual deviations and practices in which sex drugs are sometimes used'. There was no more to the story than the headline, but it gave the impression that the Bogle-

Chandler investigation had completely floundered.

That same day, the *Sunday Mirror* turned the mystery into a global human catastrophe. In an exclusive interview, party guest, John Booty-Johnson, a self-proclaimed geologist, big-game hunter and short story writer, asserted that Bogle and Mrs Chandler were not involved in a 'sordid affair' but had been murdered. He offered no reason for his murder theory, but said of Bogle:

> I heard of his death the next day with disbelief and shock. I grieved for him and his friends and his family. Today, believing he and Mrs Chandler were cleverly, vilely murdered, I grieve for the perpetrator—and for mankind, too.

That afternoon detectives Bateman and Parsons interrogated Johnson about his claim. Johnson apparently backtracked completely. The following day, he recanted the story in the press:

> This was a misstatement. It is not true. I did not say this. I have been misquoted. To my personal knowledge I have no evidence or information that would support such a definite statement.

By now it was clear that the media was setting the agenda and sending the police on 'wild goose chases' across Sydney. Aroused by profit not probity, the *Mirror*'s ambitious proprietor, Rupert Murdoch, took a direct interest in the Bogle-Chandler case. Bill Jenkings later wrote:

> He'd attend the morning editorial conferences to discuss the case and plan how we'd treat it in the upcoming editions of the paper—how we would keep knocking off the *Sun*.[26]

Australia's tabloid readers certainly lapped it up. But perhaps like no other case in recent times, the Bogle-Chandler story had turned into a media circus. The investigation itself, led by a Police Commissioner who believed in 'public relations', was being manipulated and derailed by journalists, self-publicists, conspiracy theorists and scientific profiteers.

As it transpired, Professor Thorp's cardiac experiments came up negative. His findings, he admitted, were totally consistent with 'death from natural causes'.

The case for murder was unravelling.

11. Lady Killer

Dr Bogle with staff

From the outset, Sydney's tabloids saw the bearded Geoffrey Chandler, with his 'free-sex' attitudes and bohemian connections, as fair game. Meanwhile, every section of the media eulogised Dr Bogle as a Rhodes scholar, a world-renowned physicist and a respectable family man.

A few days after the story broke, the *Mirror*'s feature writer, Gerald Stone, went to the Bogle home and discovered it had been vacated:

> Nowhere in the small square house could there be a secret. It is a house to be young and happy in, a house

> for listening to music, talking to friends, telling stories to children. Five days have not been time enough to leave a stain of sorrow on this happy house. But for Mrs Bogle it has become too bitter with memories. Her husband has now gone. Now she, too, has left it.[27]

In her only interview to the newspapers, Mrs Bogle said Gilbert was a devoted husband and father. But there were secrets in Bogle's world.

A number of women contacted detectives with claims that Dr Bogle had been involved with them or with other women. The wife of a close colleague claimed Bogle persisted in telephoning and asking her out while her husband was in the room. Another married woman revealed that Bogle posted her hand-drawn maps to entice her to a lunchtime rendezvous.

Indeed, it appears the fit, talented and gregarious Bogle saw himself as a 'lady-killer'. On one occasion, his colleague Doug Milne watched on in awe as Bogle delighted the females present by playing a tune on a piano as removalists wheeled it into the room.

> He had a lot of charm. He could say a few things in Italian and charm the pants off them, I guess. We had a lady who came along to sell encyclopaedias and Gib was so charming to her I couldn't believe it. I thought, 'Oh, I'd like to be like that'.[28]

In 2006, I tracked down a woman who knew Bogle well. She described him as 'a lover of life, who wanted to make love to the whole world'. They were both members of a choir which practised regularly on Monday nights in a Turramurra church hall. In May 1962, seven months before his death, Bogle asked her to join him for coffee after choir. She declined the offer of coffee but arranged to meet him at a cricket ground in Turramurra. They got out of their cars and sat together on a seat beside the oval. Soon after, a car passed by. A minute or so later, the car returned and stopped. A woman got out and approached them. Hysterical and sobbing, she reproached Bogle for leaving her. When Bogle asked her to go away, she threw herself on the ground. He complained that she had been following him for months. She often waited for him outside the hall where he practised with the choir and at the railway station after work. Bogle said the woman's name was Margaret Fowler.

Seven days after the deaths of Bogle and Mrs Chandler, detectives interviewed Margaret Fowler about her relationship with the physicist. Decades later her police statements were leaked to an investigative journalist. For the first time, it was revealed that the police had had another suspect in the case other than Geoffrey Chandler.

On a windy spring morning in September 1956, Bogle had been in good humour as he toured the CSIRO's gothic, stone-clad National Standards facility at Sydney University with his new boss. At the Scientific Library, directly opposite his office, he was introduced to Mrs Margaret Fowler; a slim, reserved librarian in her late 30s with melancholy eyes, curved nose and thin lips. It was a fleeting introduction, but she was attracted to Bogle immediately: his athletic build, his charming smile, and a casualness atypical of the scientists and technicians whom she usually assisted at the library desk.

Mrs Margaret Fowler

At their first morning tea together, Mrs Fowler manoeuvred the conversation to commonalities. They both lived at Turramurra on the northern train line. Bogle had studied at Oxford. She was a British-born, London University graduate of physics and mathematics. In 1952, she and her chemical engineer husband, Robert Fowler, joined a wave of British scientists migrating to Australia. Unwilling to compete in the male-dominated world of research, she took a position at the CSIRO in the scientific library. The work was tedious, but far less so than being a housewife.

Mrs Fowler made sure she had contact with Gib almost everyday and began to read his attentions as a promise of romance. One evening in 1959, they met at Turramurra Squash Courts. Afterwards, they drove to a nearby park in his car. She told him her marriage lacked intimacy and was less than satisfactory. Her husband, she said, showed no interest in her emotionally or sexually. With that cue, Bogle kissed her. That night she fell in love with him.

But the following day, at work, she realised he was in the position of power when he completely ignored her. Travelling home together on the train a few days later, he said that he suspected her to be a possessive woman. If that didn't cut deep enough, he said he was now interested in someone else. Bogle gave Mrs Fowler the impression that he had slept in more beds than a travelling salesman.

Despite Bogle's hurtful lack of romantic attachment to Margaret Fowler, their relationship became a sexual one. They first made love in his office. She was physically attractive, he said, but there was 'no personality attraction'. Future meetings were irregular and mostly at his whim. Once, while making love in his office, she told him 'You can't treat me like this.' He said, 'I only like you when you don't talk. Once you start reproaching me, I don't like you any more, and it's coming over me now and I'm going home. Get up!' Fowler slapped his face and he resumed making love to her.[29]

Occasionally, they would meet and drive to a local park and make love in a secluded location. He once told her he had had an affair with a woman in a New Zealand park. One night in 1960, Bogle drove Mrs Fowler to a park and found a private place to lie down. She told detectives, 'He was more tender than usual and he said, "This is the first time I have felt fond of you." He stroked me while we were on the ground.'

Fowler revealed to detectives the gritty details of their lovemaking. She said he was in the habit of only removing his trousers and underpants, leaving his shoes and shirt on—just like the morning he died.

What she had to gain from exposing Bogle and herself like this was anyone's guess. It wasn't a church confessional but a murder investigation. But Margaret Fowler continued on with her sordid revelations, claiming that she had come to an arrangement with her scientist husband. She could have extra-marital relations provided it did not take place within the family home. But Mrs Fowler defied her husband's wishes. One winter's evening, while her husband was out, Bogle came over and they made love on the lounge floor in front of the fireplace. Another night, they went to the bedroom, but they were tempting fate. As Bogle was getting dressed, a car pulled into the garage. Mrs Fowler panicked, 'Robert's coming, hurry up!' As Robert Fowler came in the front door, Bogle escaped via the balcony, carrying his shoes and socks. Three months later, Fowler finally confronted his wife, 'I heard Gib jump off the balcony. I heard him.'

Bogle feared he had been seen and concocted a less than convincing cover story to tell his wife should Mr Fowler turn up at the Bogle home. He said he had gone to Mrs Fowler's home in Turramurra instead of attending choir practice and that she had gone into the bedroom and thrown herself on the bed naked. He claimed he was revolted by her actions but as he went to leave, he heard a car drive into the front yard. To avoid detection in a compromising situation, he said he left by the window and slid down a pillar.

Bogle's bizarre story, which his wife allegedly verified to police, offered no explanation for being at the Fowler residence in the first place. According to surviving detectives, Mrs Bogle did not believe that he was having affairs with other women.

While working at the CSIRO, Mrs Fowler had also become acquainted with Geoffrey Chandler, who worked on the next floor.

At his second police interview, Chandler admitted that in 1953 he occasionally drove Mrs Fowler home and kissed her in his car, though he denied they had ever been intimate. He said that Mrs Fowler was at the Murraybank party the day his wife first met Dr Bogle.

She was highly emotional when discussing Bogle; admitting they had been having an affair and that he had only recently rejected her. When Bogle walked off with Mrs Chandler, Mrs Fowler alerted Geoffrey Chandler, 'He shouldn't do that, you know.' Chandler laughed, 'I think it's about fifty-fifty.'

Bogle's relationship with Mrs Fowler was torturously one-sided. She wanted love and intimacy while Bogle merely wanted sex when it suited him. Bogle informed Mrs Fowler that he had told his wife all about her; a move obviously designed to ensure she did not go to Vivienne in some jealous rage to inflict revenge for his callous treatment of her. The longer the relationship continued, the more likely that possibility became. On one occasion, when he rejected her, she threatened suicide with barbiturates.

Seven weeks prior to his death, Bogle met Margaret Fowler and said he was going to America in the New Year. She said she was returning to London, but could not envisage living without him. Bogle allegedly replied that they could have a flat together in London.

The police believed Mrs Fowler had an intense and delusional infatuation with Dr Bogle. But was it enough to suspect her of murdering Dr Bogle and Mrs Chandler? Interviewed on five occasions, without her husband present, she revealed more and more intimate details about their relationship. Robert Fowler tried to protect his wife from herself. While she was infatuated with Bogle, he said, he didn't believe she was having an intimate affair with him. This was counter to Mrs Fowler's own testimony.

Detectives investigated the Fowlers' whereabouts at New Year. They claimed they had attended a party within walking distance of their home in Turramurra between 10 pm and 4 am. As Bogle left the Nash party soon after this time, it would have been impossible for Margaret Fowler to intercept him and Mrs Chandler as they drove off from Chatswood.

Detective Ron Rudgley was one of the investigating officers:

> Dr Bogle had a sexual relationship with Mrs Fowler. Initially, we considered both her and her husband as possible suspects. But our investigation showed that she was certainly at another New Year's Eve party and she just couldn't be regarded as a suspect and neither could the husband.

If little else, Mrs Fowler revealed the extent of Dr Bogle's double-life and his modus operandi of taking women to parks to make love. Taking Mrs Chandler to the lover's lane beside the Lane Cove River, it seems, was not out of the ordinary. Indeed, he may well have taken women to the same location previously. How and why it all went wrong on New Year's morning was still to be answered.

12. Third Person

It was clear that Bogle and Chandler ended up at the Lane Cove River for one purpose. The area was a very well-known tail-light alley where lovers went for privacy. Detectives came to a number of conclusions:

- Both victims left the party soon after 4.05 am.
- At about 4.30 am Dr Bogle was seen in his car, together with a woman, in the car park near Fullers Bridge.
- Neither Dr Bogle nor Mrs Chandler was beyond taking part in extra-marital sexual associations.
- Both victims had been on the riverbed of the Lane

Cove River near where the bodies were found. At close to low tide, the muddy riverbed was relatively dry, with a carpet of she-oak needles providing protection. Three items of apparel were found in a distinct line a yard out from the riverbed, suggesting the couple lay down between the clothing and riverbank to be out of view of passers by.

- Careful examination of the victims' clothing revealed that Dr Bogle's apparel was removed without force and Mrs Chandler's dress had been removed from her shoulders voluntarily before she entered the depression where her body was found.
- There was no evidence to suggest that another person moved the victims to their final positions.
- Dr Bogle could not himself have placed his clothing over his body in the manner as found.
- They could not rule out that a 'third person'—someone who may have come across the bodies—had 'covered them as a mark of respect'.

Detective Ron Rudgley:

> Every investigator on this matter was completely convinced that there was a third person involved. Not so much as the perpetrator or the person who caused their deaths, but certainly some person must have been present to cover the bodies in the way they were.

Detectives set out to identify all the cars at the site on New Year's morning, hoping that the occupants could provide information not only about the movements of the victims but also of other visitors to the area. A number of people telephoned the police and endured intense questioning as to why they were at the river.

At 7.30 pm, on the day of the deaths, a Mr Roberts from Lane Cove telephoned Chatswood detectives. He said he had seen Dr Bogle and the woman in a Prefect car that morning but ended the call before giving his contact details. Attempts to trace the caller were unsuccessful.

Four days later, at exactly the same time, a male caller stated that he had driven along the track where the victims were found and he had seen a man there. The caller was asked to come into the Police Station and make a statement.

The man identified himself as Raymond Challis, of Rushcutters Bay, on the eastern side of the city. The short, one-armed, former carpenter in his mid-30s wore dark spectacles and perspired heavily under questioning. Detectives told him that his Ford Escort had been identified both parked near the entrance of the bush track and driving along it. He told detectives that he had left his home at 3.30 am and drove to the Lane Cove River at 4 am. After a walk along the bush track to the golf links, he returned to his car, parked at the entrance to the track. After about 20 minutes, he got out of the car and walked along Lady Game Drive, which runs parallel to the river, and past the dusty tail-light alley between the bridge and the weir. On the way, he said, a car fitting the description of Dr Bogle's Ford Prefect pulled up along side him. It was around 4.35 am, he estimated. The driver of the Prefect, he claimed, went to speak to him, but for some reason decided against it. Challis walked on some distance. Later, he returned to his car again and saw Dr Bogle's car now parked closer to Fullers Bridge.

Detectives assumed Challis' presence might have caused Bogle to move his car. Asked why he decided to go the Lane Cove River at that time of the morning, in the dark, Challis said he usually went there to collect soil and shrubs for his garden or to exercise his dog.

But the police were suspicious of his motives. Under interrogation, Challis admitted that he was there to 'tout' on couples making love in the area. He admitted driving his car down the bush track where the bodies were later found, but claimed he didn't see the couple, dead or alive. Almost as an afterthought, he said he did see a broad-shouldered, blondish-haired man in his 40s jump from the bushes in front of his car and disappear down the riverbank. But by now the police were sceptical of everything Challis said. Under further pressure, he admitted that he had called Chatswood Police Station on 1 January under the assumed name of 'Mr Roberts of Lane Cove'. Asked why he didn't mention the blondish-haired man the first time he called, he shrugged and said it had slipped his mind.

Detectives could not establish the identity of the blond man and doubted that he even existed. When they put it to Challis that he had covered the victims, he emphatically denied even seeing the bodies. Everything about Challis rang warning bells: not only his colourless, dissociative persona and naked obfuscations, but also his attempts to hide his disability by placing the remainder of his left arm in the side pocket of his trousers.

The question was: Could he have covered the bodies? Detective Ron Rudgley had his doubts:

> Now, so far as covering up the bodies, I would doubt that Challis is the person responsible mainly because he has one arm and I would feel that while a one-armed person could have put the beer cartons over Mrs Chandler, he would have had a great lot of difficulty putting the clothes over Dr Bogle in the manner that they were found.[30]

Soon there was another suspect. A local resident contacted the police saying he saw a green and white Ford Customline sedan parked in the area. When the media broadcast a description of the distinctive car, its owner, Edwin Harold Batiste, contacted police. The master butcher and greyhound trainer from Hunters Hill told detectives he had exercised his racing dogs on the nearby golf course that morning. He said he crossed Fullers Bridge at 4.33 am. He recalled seeing Dr Bogle's car in the parking area, but not the occupants. He then drove onto the upper bush track to a local park, from where he walked his dogs down to the golf links. Batiste claimed he did not go along the lower bush track where the victims died. His delay in contacting the police raised suspicions. But the greyhound trainer emphatically denied seeing Bogle and Chandler, dead or alive.

But Ron Rudgley always considered Eddy Batiste the most likely 'third person':

One thing that makes me think this is that the dogs have a wonderful sense of smell, thousands of times better than ours. If Batiste was there alongside of the river the dogs may have sniffed the bodies out. But like all the other aspects of this case we were only working on supposition.[31]

13. Inquest

Geoffrey Chandler at the Inquest

By the end of April, the police had received over 1,000 letters from the public offering either information or theories. Filed away also were dozens of letters from police and scientific agencies across Australia and around the world, which had been contacted in search of similar cases. There were typed statements of the more than 200 people interviewed. The police running sheet of the investigation alone ran to 770 pages. And it all added up to a riddle inside a mystery.

On 7 May 1963, the Coronial Inquest began with expectations high that the Coroner would deliver a solution.

The grand sandstone façade of the Central Court of Petty Sessions in Liverpool Street, Sydney belied its cramped collection of uninviting, timber-lined courtrooms. In the recently remodelled Court 3, 20 journalists and people in the public gallery stood as Coroner Jack Loomes took his seat beneath the coat of arms. Many of those in the packed gallery would come day after day, desperate to see in the flesh the players, who were now household names.

Over the next three weeks, more than 50 witnesses would appear. Throughout, Loomes would present a sober approach to the proceedings. Devoid of emotion, without affectation or even mannerisms, he would speak in an even, gentle way, particularly to female witnesses.

Seated at a long table below the witness dock, were the legal representatives of the Bogle, Chandler and Morphett families and, assisting the Coroner, the tall, formidable Sergeant Goode.

The first witnesses called, the party hosts, Ken and Ruth Nash, were almost celebrities. Early in the case their photos had appeared regularly in newspapers.

The Court listened intently to the make-up of their invitation list and the comings and goings and attitudes of the guests, particularly the victims. Of intense interest were details of Geoffrey Chandler's absence from the party during the night and how he left the party twice without his wife. While offering nothing in the way of new information, the couple merely reaffirmed the prejudices already established by the press that the Chandlers were outsiders and the dashing, talented and ever ebullient scientist, Dr Gilbert Bogle, was the 'life of the party' who could do little wrong.

But Ken Nash gave a conflicting account about a fundamental piece of evidence. In his original statement to the police, Nash said he witnessed Dr Bogle and Mrs Chandler embracing on the back lawn. In the witness box, under oath, he said he saw them together in the backyard, but denied seeing 'any undue friendliness between Dr Bogle and Mrs Chandler'.

'Partly in jest, from a point of puckish humour', he said, 'I switched off the light, which spilt on the lawn. They returned to the house immediately.'

Surely Sergeant Goode had access to Nash's police statement. Why he let Nash downplay what happened in the backyard is open to speculation.

Earlier that morning, during his opening address, the Coroner had said that the only evidence he might suppress would be anything he 'considered against the interests of decency'.

The next day, the Coroner allowed the press its first glimpse of Dr Bogle's mysterious artwork. The secrecy surrounding it had caused the media to speculate that it had something to do with the deaths or was pornographic.

Reporters were decidedly underwhelmed by his Picasso-style depiction of a double-faced woman with a severed right hand and left foot, cut off just above the ankle.

The Coroner then heard testimonies from the party guests who invariably described the evening as 'sedate' and 'sober'. Moustachioed Jack Booty-Johnson, who had previously embarrassed the police with his media speculation that the victims had been murdered, said that he did not believe Bogle was the type of man who would have committed suicide. He testified that toward the end of the evening he had heard voices coming from the vicinity of the cars parked outside the Nash home, but could not identify the voices as male or female.

Other guests testified that as the evening progressed there was no noticeable change in either Dr Bogle's or Mrs Chandler's demeanour. The only exception was musician James Day-Hakkar, who had arrived late to the party at 3 am. He had told police that he did notice a change in Dr Bogle; from a breezy, talkative person at 3 am to one who was very tired or very sick by the time he left the party about an hour later. Under cross-examination, Day-Hakkar attempted to recant this opinion; admitting that he was not a good judge, having only met Dr Bogle for the first time that evening and for little more than an hour.

The following day, the Inquest convened on the banks of the Lane Cove River. Reporters and photographers were forced to stay out of earshot of the Coroner, legal counsel and detectives, but within a few days newsreel audiences across Australia would finally get to see the infamous rubbish-strewn location, made all the more dismal by heavy rain.

Day after day, intense public and media interest in the case meant a crowded court. People queued for hours hoping to secure one of the 35 seats available. On the steps, press photographers jostled for the best position to snap the witnesses arriving. The fashionable Ruth Nash, who attended every day of the Inquest, quickly became a favourite of the editors. The *Daily Mirror* featured her on the front page wearing a smart twin-set and hat, under the banner 'Mrs. Nash's Hats—continued'. The caption read: 'Fourth hat, fourth day: Mrs. Ruth Nash, hostess at the fateful New Year's party, chose a brown fur today.'

Next in the witness box were the two youths who had discovered Dr Bogle's body. Dressed in a coat and tie, and now with longer, slicked-down hair, Michael McCormick had lost his schoolboy looks. He said he had come across the man laying beside the Lane Cove River and thought he was a hobo 'sleeping it off'.

'I looked at him and saw his face was turning blue; it didn't look right.'

He said he walked off along the track to the Chatswood golf links where he met a friend and went looking for golf balls. About an hour later, he said, he came back along the bush track where the man was lying, had a 'further look' and saw that his face 'had gone darker'. The friend, Dennis Wheway, said, 'I noticed his nose was purple. There was a small trickle of blood from his nose and mouth.'

Sergeant Goode, assisting the Coroner, questioned both teenagers about Dr Bogle's body. They confirmed that it had been draped with his trousers and coat, but it looked as if he was wearing them. Between the coat and the man's white shirt was a mat made of carpet.

The next witness, kiosk proprietor Geoffrey Little, said he inspected the body before calling the police and agreed with the boys' description of placement of the clothing. A war veteran, Mr Little said he had seen other dead bodies. The Coroner asked, 'In death was there any peculiar manifestations in his body that you had not seen before?' He replied that the only thing he had not noticed on other dead bodies was a purplish band running down from Dr Bogle's forehead to his nose.

Not since the tragic Graeme Thorne kidnapping and murder case of 1961 had there been such public interest shown in a Coronial Inquest. The newspapers milked every detail. On the fourth day, the *Sun* dedicated its first five pages to the story. It had everything—even a one-armed man! Kenneth George Challis said that he saw Bogle's car pull up. The driver, he said, 'looked white, paler than a normal man'.

Sergeant Goode questioned him at length about his story to the police concerning the mysterious blond man who jumped out in front of his car. Challis said it all happened in a split second and could not offer much else about him other than he 'was fairly well-built, yellow hair, rather long hair, T-shirt and trousers.'

There was no probing of Challis' reason for being there—to spy on lovers. He did admit, however, that he had earlier walked along the bush track beside the river and on hearing a car coming ducked down in the bush. Asked why, he said, 'I just didn't want to be seen. People might get the wrong impression. If you saw me there, unshaven, with a dirty shirt, at four o'clock in the morning, what would you think?'

But as days slipped by, and witness after witness offered less than illuminating testimony, the *Sunday Telegraph* reported:

> No one was any the wiser about what happened to Dr Bogle and Mrs Chandler in those fateful hours until the time their bodies were found in mysterious circumstances... But the lack of a real sensation has not robbed the Inquest of its interest. Rumours continually sweep the public and Press benches of 'mystery witnesses' to appear.

Legal counsel representing the families pressed the Coroner to bring forward the scientific evidence regarding the victims, but Mr Loomes argued that he ran the Inquest and was going to present evidence in 'chronological order': first the party; then the discovery of the bodies; and then the testimony of the police, etc.

Coroner Jack Loomes

Sergeant Andrews, one of the first officers at the scene, was easily the most impressive witness to enter the stand. He recounted with attention to detail how Bogle's body was covered and how it appeared to be done in such a way as to provide maximum warmth and protection. He added that the position Mrs Chandler was found in was easily accessible from the riverbed. Her shoes and panties, and Dr Bogle's belt were also found on the riverbed.

Detective Sergeant George Lindsay of the CIB Scientific Branch told the Coroner that there was no sign of a struggle at the crime scene. Stains on Bogle's clothing and shoes suggested he had used both heels and elbows to get from the riverbed up onto the bank. Mrs Chandler's clothing and body had various stains. Two knee impressions were found on the mudflats, which matched the netting material of her slip.

When the officer in charge of the Scientific Branch, Detective Sergeant Allan Clarke, gave evidence the proceedings became more combative. Clarke theorised that it was Mrs Chandler who had covered Dr Bogle 'to keep him warm'. Stirred by what he considered creative fancy, Kevin Murray, Geoffrey Chandler's legal representative argued there was 'nothing by way of substantive fact' to support such a theory.

'It reduces itself to this,' Murray said, 'because you cannot or have not been able to find any sign of a third person, it must have been Margaret Chandler who covered Dr Bogle's body. For all you know Mrs Chandler may have been covered with cartons and was lying in the depression before Dr Bogle was covered.

Tell me just one fact to controvert that?'

Minutes of intense argument with the witness followed. In the end, Chandler's lawyer suggested that it was 'very embarrassing to the police' that no 'third person' had been found. Legal counsel for both Geoffrey Chandler and the Bogle family made it clear that they had no faith in the Scientific Branch's hypothesis of the events.

One of the leading detectives on the case, Detective Sergeant Parsons, was also questioned on this theory. He said he thought it possible that Mrs Chandler had covered herself with the three cardboard beer cartons. Equally, he said, someone else may have done it. On cross examination, he agreed that having regard for a woman's modesty 'and had she been able to', she would have more likely corrected her clothing rather than cover herself in such a way.

At the start of the third week, the Inquest finally came to the much-anticipated presentation of the pathology and toxicology reports. Dr Laing, the Director of the NSW Division of Forensic Medicine, said he had made an external and internal examination of the bodies of Dr Bogle and Mrs Chandler. In both victims, he said, he could not determine whether the breathing stopped because of heart failure or whether the heart stopped because breathing had failed. The only thing he could deduce was that both victims had died of the same cause:

> First, of course is the fact that what killed one, killed the other. We have established that rigor mortis was well developed in the case of Dr Bogle; we find that he died

> as far back as allowable and that is shortly after he was seen alive—at 5 am, on 1 January. In the case of Mrs Chandler, these appearances were not as advanced, and this gives the impression that she could have died an hour or two later than Dr Bogle.

He admitted though that they might have died around the same time. The disparity may have been caused by the way the bodies were covered.

Close inspection of the bodies revealed no signs of hypodermic needle punctures. Strangulation could be ruled out because there were no signs of injury to the necks. Moreover, vomiting would not have occurred if a person had been strangled. Dr Laing said tests were carried out for funnel web spider venom and radioactivity and they had both proved negative.

Sergeant Goode assisting the Coroner

Mr Ernest 'Sammy' Ogg, the NSW Government Analyst, said that his department tested the organs of the victims as well as the food and drink from the Nash party. After four months of laboratory analysis, 'The net result showed nothing in the organs of Dr Bogle or Mrs Chandler which indicated the presence of any poisonous substance.' Asked whether he thought there was any prospect of the mystery being solved, Mr Ogg relayed that he held out no prospect of the mystery being solved by chemical analysis.

Toxicologist Vivian Mahoney, who had spent months of concentrated effort searching for the poison in the blood and tissues of the victims, agreed that the investigation had met with no success in establishing the cause of the deaths.

Controversy erupted when Professor Roland Thorp, who had carried out experiments with samples of the victim's tissue on animal hearts, entered the witness box. Thorp also admitted he had no success, but blamed the delay between the discovery of the bodies and the ultimate commencement of the analysis for the failure to find the cause of death. Doctor Laing countered, suggesting that Professor Thorp was himself on holidays and did not consider the matter of sufficient urgency to prevent him from completing his leave.

Dr Cameron Cramp, from the Division of Forensic Medicine, then presented his findings concerning swabs of the victims and microscopic investigation of their clothing. He said tests on Margaret Chandler had failed to find any evidence of sexual intercourse. But the Coroner stopped Mr Cramp from presenting further evidence, invoking Section 42 of the Coroner's Act. The suppression of this evidence was frustrating to the media. It also suggested some sort of cover up on the grounds of 'decency'.

Following the disappointing police and scientific evidence, the Coroner turned his attention to the victims and their relationships. The most anticipated witness was the elusive Geoffrey Chandler. His attempt to avoid press photographers by entering the court via an underground tunnel was thwarted by police.

Shielding his face from photographers, Chandler entered via the front door of the Court and looked every bit the guilty man. The previous week, his lawyer had worked with him, training his nerves against a volley of personal questions that would surely come his way. But in the witness box, Chandler looked and sounded nervous. The Coroner would ask him continually to speak up.

But compared with all the witnesses before him, Geoffrey Chandler spoke in absolutes and did not obfuscate either about his relationship with Pamela Logan or Margaret's attraction to Gilbert Bogle. He said that Margaret originally met Dr Bogle at a Murraybank party on 21 December and was entranced by him:

> In discussion between Margaret and myself about the Murraybank party, she gave the opinion that of the people present Dr Bogle was the most interesting and that she felt quite an attraction towards him. She said the thought of going to bed with him was attractive. She put this in the same way as one might describe owning a Rolls Royce.

Chandler then described the events of New Year's Eve; arriving at the Nash party, leaving for Balmain where he met Pamela Logan, accompanying her to her bed-sit in Darlington and then his return to the Chatswood party. Of his final minutes with Margaret at the party he said: 'Margaret evidenced no indication of coming with me when I wished to leave, which suggested to me she wished to stay a little longer.'

Chandler said he sat in his car outside the Nash home smoking a cigarette, before driving away. He explained with obvious regret: 'I felt I had inadvertently left Margaret in the lurch and that she might have decided after all to accompany me home.'

On his return to his Croydon home with the children at about 10.30 am, he found she was not at home. He thought she must have already been there and gone for a drive with Dr Bogle. He said he made no enquiries as to her whereabouts, because he had no reason to be alarmed.

Chandler's claim that he expected Dr Bogle and his wife to drive to his Croydon home to have intercourse, sparked strong argument between the Bogle legal representative, Mr Ward, and Sergeant Goode. Implicit in Goode's questioning was that Chandler's so-called 'arrangement' with his wife implied that she would have sex with Dr Bogle. But Mr Ward said that Mr Chandler was using this as an excuse for his own behaviour: 'If the excuse he gives drags down the credit of other people or could drag down their credit when it is only this man's opinion or excuse, it goes past the realms of hearsay.'

'I feel there is a good deal of merit in the your objection, Mr Ward.' Coroner Loomes responded.

'It is of value of the Court,' argued Sgt Goode, 'to know what a person as closely linked as Chandler is to one of the deceased would say. It was of value to

Pamela Logan (left) at the Inquest

know it if he had spoken to both deceased on what arrangements there were as far as he was concerned.'

'I feel I would be going far beyond the rules of evidence to allow the witness to give an expectation of what he thought was going to happen,' countered Coroner Loomes.

The argument over the word 'arrangement', and Chandler's 'expectations' continued for many minutes and denied the simple reality that Bogle and Mrs Chandler were found half-naked in a lovers' lane. It was the second example of the suppression of facts relating to Dr Bogle's reputation in as many days and set a pattern that would continue throughout the Inquest.

In contrast, a great deal of time was spent dissecting

Geoffrey Chandler's affair with Pamela Logan. Logan had provided his alibi, and while it was never said outright, it was implied that the affair might have provided a motive for Chandler to kill his wife.

Of interest to the Coroner was his continued relationship with Logan after the death of his wife. The Coroner asked how long before he saw Miss Logan again. Chandler suggested three weeks. Coroner Loomes knew differently: 'Mr Chandler, this was a great tragedy, a great blow to you?'

'Yes.'

'Two days after (the deaths), on Thursday, do you remember meeting Mr Anthony Morphett, your brother-in-law, who accompanied you to a hotel in Newtown?'

'I recollect meeting him, I don't remember what period of time elapsed.'

'He said you took him to a house in Annandale and introduced him to a girl named Pam Logan, whom you had told him earlier that day was your girlfriend?'

'I don't doubt it, but I have no recollection of it...I do not think I used the word "girlfriend" [with] which the term is normally associated.'

Chandler did himself no favours. He painted himself as a man who had little respect for his dead wife or her family. He also came across as a man who simply did not care what the world thought.

Sedately dressed in a plain black frock, white gloves and pearls, the beautiful Pamela Logan raised heckles from a gaggle of curious Sydney matrons as she entered the Court.

A disapproving hum from the public gallery continued as she stepped into the witness box. The Coroner told Logan that the atmosphere of the courtroom might be unfamiliar to her and if she needed to rest to tell him.

Sergeant Goode opened the questioning: 'You knew Geoffrey Arnold Chandler?'

'Yes.'

'You had known him for some time before January 1?

'Yes, for six to eight months.'

'For some of that period it would be fair to say you and Geoffrey Chandler had formed a close association?'

'Yes.'

'He saw you frequently, and apart from work?'

'Yes.'

'You knew he was married?'

'Yes.'

Goode then explored Logan's recollection of the evening, from Chandler's arrival at the Balmain party to picking up the Chandler children in the morning: 'Did he tell you he had asked Dr Bogle to take his wife home, that he had told Dr Bogle not to worry about the children that he would look after them, and that he wanted you to go with him to Granville, get the children and bring them back to your place?'

'Yes.'

For those in the gallery hoping for further salacious revelations, Logan's time in the witness box was disappointingly short. There was nothing presented to implicate either Logan or Geoffrey Chandler in the deaths. Cool and dignified, she left the Court and allegedly made arrangements to leave the country.

Monday, 27 May held the promise of a sensation. A mystery witness was to be called. A crowd had queued for hours: some people bearing thermos flasks and cut sandwiches.

Dressed in an apricot frock and a high-crowned black velour hat trimmed with fur, the 'mystery woman', Mrs Margaret Fowler, appeared nervous as she took the oath. She had good reason to be. But before questioning could begin, her lawyer protested to the Coroner that Mrs Fowler's testimony was not relevant. Mr Ward, representing the Bogle family, agreed. He told the Coroner that all counsel had been informed of the general nature of the proposed evidence:

> Whatever Mrs Fowler could say would be irrelevant to the inquiry. What she might say would only tend to distress and embarrass strangers to this Inquest and persons who are not even associated with the events of that night.

The Coroner adjourned the inquest for 20 minutes. Waiting outside, another 'mystery witness', Bill Berry, spoke nervously with his lawyer. Berry was Margaret Chandler's former lover. On his return, the Coroner told the court:

> Mrs Fowler's evidence could not help me in any way in the charge that has been placed upon me to determine the manner and cause of the deaths of the deceased. The reasons I have given for not requiring this witness to give evidence also apply to the witness William James Berry.

The Coroner stood down both witnesses to protect both the families of the victims and the public morality.

The longest Inquest in the state's history had all but come to an end, not with a bang, but a whimper. Fifty witnesses, including some of the country's most distinguished pathologists, and not one skerrick of evidence had been presented to suggest how the couple had died. In his final statement, Mr Loomes admitted the system had failed the victims and their families: 'I find it hard to believe that I am no more able today to ascertain the manner and cause of death than I was when the inquiry began.'

Without judgment, speculation or histrionics, he admitted:

Coroner bars woman's evidence

STRANGERS MAY SUFFER: COUNSEL

> As this court is not a court of morals, neither do I intend to offer any comment on certain evidence placed before me. There is one thing, however, that I feel I can say with absolute certainty–that each of these unfortunate persons died an unnatural death.

The failure of the police, scientists and the coroner to identify a cause of death of Dr Bogle and Mrs Chandler inevitably led to questions about the thoroughness of their investigations. Were the autopsies carried out too late? Was the scientific equipment used up to date? Did information withheld at the Inquest hold the secret to their deaths?

In smoke-filled hotels around CIB headquarters, reporters sidled up to detectives to grill them about the two mystery witnesses. It was pretty clear there were some disappointed investigators, but it wasn't

Ruth and Ken Nash

in any detective's interest to whisper or cast off their frustrations into a reporter's ear, just yet. But many detectives were furious with the Police Commissioner, Norman Allan. His strategy of feeding the media with too many stories about nonsensical leads had seriously backfired.

With a murderer still possibly on the loose and sensing the media and public's dismay, Commissioner Allan called yet another press conference. He said his detectives would 'continue to pursue every avenue of investigation in an effort to find out how Bogle and Chandler died.' No unsolved case, he said, 'is ever marked "closed" and the files are always available for review.'

Since 1945, there had been only 11 other unsolved major mysteries in the state of New South Wales, but this case, Commissioner Allan admitted, was 'the mystery of the century'.

14. Red Herring

Conus geographus

A week after the Coroner's Inquest, the case took an unexpected turn and Geoffrey Chandler was back in the frame for murder. Detectives received a letter from a 37-year-old Brisbane University zoologist who claimed that he knew of a poison that could have killed Dr Bogle and Mrs Chandler.

Dr Robert Endean explained that his laboratory was expert in toxins from the shellfish, *Conus geographus*. In the wrong hands, he wrote, these toxins could be used as a murder weapon. The symptoms they deliver to a victim seemed to match the descriptions in the media.

When he wrote the letter, Dr Endean didn't know that his 23-year-old researcher, Clara Berry, was married to Margaret Chandler's former lover, Bill Berry, one of the two witnesses stood down at the Inquest.

It was a stunning connection, which detectives believed had to be more than coincidence.

Sensing a breakthrough, senior CIB detectives, Don Fergusson and John Bateman flew to Queensland to interview Mrs Berry. Despite her youth, Clara was as knowledgeable as anyone in Australia about *Conus* poisons. Her research involved thirty different species, five of which are extremely venomous. Under Endean's tutorage, she had perfected a method of extracting *Conus* venom. At first, the young researcher didn't realise that the police were sizing her up as a possible suspect.

> Dr Endean was rather shocked when I told him that the Chandlers had been friends of ours. Detectives came and interviewed me. I was really pretty upset that they should be suspecting cone shells being involved in this. They said, 'Is it possible to kill someone with it?' And I said, 'Well I don't think so because you can't just dose somebody's drink with it. It's unstable. You would have to carry it around in a thermos flask, frozen, and then you'd have to ask the victims to hold still while you injected it into them. You wouldn't actually expect it to have any effect if it was eaten. A lot of poisons are like that.'

The police contacted airline companies and discovered that someone by the name of 'G. Chandler' had travelled from Sydney to Brisbane a few weeks prior to the Bogle and Chandler deaths. Geoffrey Chandler denied that he had travelled to Brisbane.

Dr John Laing, who had carried out the Bogle and Chandler autopsies, joined the detectives in Brisbane to investigate the cone fish breakthrough. He returned to Sydney with samples of toxin for testing against the victims' tissues. ABC television filmed the preparation of the samples. The tests, Laing said, would take ten days to complete. Meanwhile, a rumour circulated in the press that a quantity of the cone fish poison was missing from Dr Endean's laboratory. The police denied the rumour, but detectives Bateman and Fergusson had ascertained that some of the toxin was missing and Mrs Berry was the person responsible for its safekeeping.

Dr Laing, however, started to have serious doubts about the whole business. He believed that there was nothing to support Endean's claim that cone fish poison could kill humans; his experiments had only been carried out in mice. Ten days later, the Government Analyst released the much-awaited results of their toxicology tests. They were negative.

Conus geographus toxin was yet another theory added to the 'if only' list.

For Clara Berry, the incident marked the beginning of the end of her promising career:

> The next thing I heard it was in the media somewhere that they discounted the possibility of cone shells having being involved and that was the end of it. But Endean

> himself got a bit funny and he wouldn't let me into the room where my specimens were kept until he was there. I wasn't given a key to my own specimens. And he became unfriendly afterwards. Eventually, I lost the job and didn't finish my Masters. I have always felt that he did that [going to the police] more as a way of promoting his research rather than because he really thought it was [the poison that killed Bogle and Chandler]. He was a real media tart and used to get himself into the media as much as possible because that was a way of getting research grants.

It was a familiar story.

◆ ◆ ◆

In the ensuing years, both the NSW Police and Dr Laing received correspondence from other scientists offering their expertise in solving the crime. One such letter came from Professor John Cleland, the most respected and decorated pathologist South Australia had produced.

Born in 1878, Cleland had obtained his Bachelor of Medicine at the University of Adelaide and his doctorate at Sydney University. From 1920 until his retirement in 1948, he was an esteemed Professor of Pathology at the University of Adelaide.

Near the end of his career, while a member of the South Australian Central Board of Health, Cleland became concerned about a poison that could leave no trace. In the hands of a cunning murderer, he surmised, it could deliver the prefect crime.

The toxin was sodium fluoroacetate, which occurs naturally in a wide range of African, Brazilian and Australian plant species, including acacias, which still grace many gardens across the nation.

In the mid-1940s sodium fluoroacetate was introduced for rodent and feral animal control under the name '1080'. Distributed around an area of infestation, baits laced with odourless and tasteless poison decimate the problem species. Relatively fast acting, some animal species suffer an excruciating death. Controversially, insects and other animals that feed on the baits or the carcasses also perish. For this reason, many countries banned the poison, but in Australia in the 1960s the use of 1080 was still widespread.

In humans, the symptoms of poisoning normally appear between 30 minutes and three hours after exposure. Initial symptoms typically include nausea, vomiting and abdominal pain. In significant poisoning, cardiac abnormalities and neurological effects appear, including muscle twitching and seizures. After a few hours, consciousness becomes progressively impaired leading to coma. Death is normally due to ventricular arrhythmias, progressive hypotension unresponsive to treatment, and secondary lung infections.

Cleland wrote to the NSW Commissioner of Police telling them of his long held concerns about 1080 'on account of the great difficulty in proving its presence if used for felonious purposes'.

In relation to the Bogle-Chandler deaths, he said, 'I think it therefore not unreasonable to assume that it may actually have been used in this case. No other likely poison can be suggested. It would help in unraveling this case if the ease with which 1080 could be obtained in NSW at the time be stated.'

Professor Cleland imagined two scenarios. Perhaps Bogle and Chandler stopped the car to go to the toilet in the bush and while doing so used something laced with the poison to clean themselves. It was a convoluted, improbable theory that revealed no understanding of Bogle and Chandler's purpose in visiting the lovers' lane.

The second scenario pointed an accusatorial finger at Mrs Chandler. Firstly, Cleland questioned whether the CSIRO was involved in work with 1080. He then suggested that 'discreet questions be asked as to whether Mrs Chandler had ever mentioned 1080 to her colleagues, or heard them discussing it.'

In this, he assumes incorrectly that Mrs Chandler worked for the CSIRO. In fact, it was her husband Geoffrey who worked for the research organisation, as did Dr Bogle.

Proving 1080 was the poison that killed Bogle and Chandler was problematic because it was theoretically undetectable. Plus, there were no known cases of human deaths. Cleland corresponded with a scientist in London who had investigated the sudden death of a young man from a compound related to 1080—organic fluorine. At autopsy, the victim's heart muscle showed 'necrotic foci', meaning that some of the heart tissue was dead. It was a possible lead, which he passed on to Dr Laing in Sydney.[32]

Laing replied that he had 're-sectioned heart blocks from Bogle and Chandler' and they 'did not demonstrate necrotic foci'. Laing added that the Government Analyst had specifically searched for 1080 in the organs of the victims and was 'certain that this substance was not present'.[33]

Cleland persisted with his intriguing 1080 theory, believing that 'not finding it may not necessarily mean that it was not administered'. But in 1968, the Commissioner of Police reiterated the Analysts' findings and said that while grateful for his interest, he could see 'no good purpose in seeking advice' from the Government Analyst.[34]

Professor Cleland finally abandoned the 1080 theory in 1969 after reading Geoffrey Chandler's book, *So You Think I Did It*?[35]

Chandler's admission that he expected Margaret and Dr Bogle to have a sexual liaison that night sparked another more salacious theory in Cleland's mind—death from 'an accidental overdose of an aphrodisiac'.[36] He imagined that Mrs Chandler had given the drug to Dr Bogle 'to stimulate sexual activities'. But then something went terribly wrong:

> It is possible that, when Mrs Chandler found she had unintentionally given a fatal dose, she had enough of the material left to take some herself.

Cleland's scenario has echoes of Shakespeare's evocative story of the star-crossed lovers, Romeo and Juliet. But he based his hypothesis on suggestions made at the Inquest that Mrs Chandler may have died a little later than Dr Bogle and that it was she who caringly covered Dr Bogle's body before dying herself.

As it was, the Government Analyst had exhaustively explored the aphrodisiac theory when a Sydney tabloid newspaper first postulated it in 1963.

The idea that Mrs Chandler was in the habit of priming men she had just met with aphrodisiacs didn't fit the image the police had pieced together of the shy young mother from Croydon Park. Of the two victims, it was Dr Bogle who had the far more extensive sexual history. Perhaps, because Bogle was an internationally respected scientist, Cleland could not conceive of him as anything other than a victim.

In another letter to the NSW Police, he pressed for information about Mrs Chandler:

> Of what religious persuasion was Mrs Chandler? If she were a good member of some Church, it would be unlikely of her to undertake this premeditated crime... Was there any mental instability in blood relations? The result of these enquiries could strengthen or lessen the likelihood of her being responsible for the deaths.... If Mrs Chandler committed the deed it must have been premeditated and I must assume that it was due to annoyance and regret that Dr Bogle was going away, which I think it was.[37]

In 1969, at the age of 91, Professor Cleland wrote to the Police Commissioner, Norman Allan, for the last time:

> Almost complete blindness has recently overtaken me and this has given me time to sum up my opinion on the

> Bogle-Chandler case. A good clinician is one who comes to a correct diagnosis on imperfect data. Doubtless you and your staff have formed your own conclusion, which may or may not be the same as mine, and if the same, some of my points may give added force to some of yours. If, for instance, you conclude as I have that Mrs Chandler was probably the culprit, it would be horrible to think, supposing that she was not, that she had been thus incriminated.[38]

Alas, imperfect data had not delivered a correct diagnosis. The Assistant Commissioner of Police responded, thanking Professor Cleland: 'Your interest in this matter is appreciated.' And that was where Cleland bowed out, some two years before his death.[39]

In Dr Laing's correspondence with Professor Cleland, he admitted dismay at his own inability to make a breakthrough:

> The various points you raise were gone into by various people, but it still left me without the one vital answer—the cause of death. If we had that, then we could go on to consider the question of accident, suicide, or murder more satisfactorily. I can supply the Coroner with plenty of theory and speculation but naturally he wants facts and proof, and those I cannot give ... I have never had so much done on a body before or since and come up with so little.[40]

To the chagrin of the scientists and police involved, the void of 'facts and proof' was about to be filled with even more extraordinary speculation—speculation that would catapult the Bogle-Chandler case yet again to the front line of the Cold War.

15. Conspiracy

Dr Bogle in his laboratory

Five days after her husband's death Vivienne Bogle told a reporter, 'My husband, Gilbert, was framed.' When the whole mysterious tragedy was cleared up, she said, he would be shown to be innocent of any dubious behaviour.

Mrs Bogle implied that the brilliant physicist had been murdered because of his scientific work. A few days later, the *Daily Mirror* exploited the idea with its 'Death Ray' story. Other newspapers, too, believed it was a strange coincidence that Bogle was killed just as he was about to leave for America to carry on his highly technical Maser research for Bell Laboratories; a powerful defence technology supplier to the US government.

It was, after all, the height of the Cold War. Only ten weeks earlier, the world had come close to global nuclear war over the Cuban Missile Crisis. And it was espionage and the illicit trade in scientific secrets that had helped bring the world to the flash point.

Australia was not immune from nuclear-charged espionage dramas. Throughout the previous decade, Australia had hosted twelve British atomic bomb tests and had partnered with Britain in a top-secret rocket project, at Woomera in South Australia. Australia was therefore of interest to Soviet spies. Only two days before Bogle and Chandler died, a major spy case, dubbed the 'Skripov Affair', played out in the streets of Adelaide and was allegedly related to both defence programs.

Daily Mirror reporter Gerald Stone:

> This was an atmosphere in which you could ferment so many different theories. It's easy to look back and say these people were very naïve and how could they have thought that and this. But the truth was that the world was in ferment.

The police received scores of letters pointing to Cold War assassination. One such letter from a Russian émigré to Australia arrived early in the investigation. He claimed there were Soviet agents within the CSIRO who were responsible for the deaths:

> The deaths could be attributed to a gang attempt on the lives of eminent scientists of Australia—an act of a specially formed terrorist block of CSIRO career employees and workers. Having great experience in criminal and political investigation work during the time of the last World War, I dare say that I can even declare with certainty that matters are not all well in the CSIRO. Russian espionage has its people there. I think that the killing of Dr Bogle is the work of CSIRO workers who have sold themselves to Russian Communism.

The writer alleged that the murders were carried out by using a spray pistol of toxic substances, or by way of closing the respiratory organs with a soft cloth or by pulling a plastic bag over the head. Such a method of killing, he said, offered the criminal world a possibility of concealing the traces of the crime and of confusing the investigation authorities in Australia. The author didn't reveal how he knew about such things. The Police sent a copy of his letter to police agencies around the country and internationally. Those that did reply suggested the author was not of sound mind.

The conspiracy mill fired up again in 1982 when someone connected to the case gave the *National Times* details of Bogle's relationship with Mrs Margaret Fowler, the mystery woman stood down at the Coronial Inquest. The story claimed the former CSIRO scientific librarian's husband, Robert Fowler, a Chief Chemical Engineer at the University of NSW, was jealous of Bogle and had used an undetectable chemical to kill him.

Why Mrs Chandler was also killed was never explained.

Rumours then spread that Fowler's university laboratory was carrying out covert research into chemical weapons. The lab was set up by the British-born Vice-Chancellor of the university, Sir Philip Baxter—an outspoken advocate for chemical, nuclear and biological weapons. In 1965, in his role as Chairman of the Australian Atomic Energy Commission, Baxter set up a uranium enrichment facility at the nuclear Lucas Heights research establishment, allegedly without the approval of the Australian government or the knowledge of the United States. Enrichment is the vital step required to build nuclear weapons and the use of this technology by 'rogue nations' has become a trigger for military action in recent times.

Whether or not Robert Fowler fitted into Baxter's grand plan is unknown. Detectives interviewed both

CSIRO building, which housed Bogle and Chandler's laboratories

Fowler and his wife over the Bogle Chandler deaths. They said they were at a New Year's party close to their home in Turramurra all evening. Their alibis, which were backed by witnesses, appeared watertight. Investigators finally discounted any connection to the events of New Year's morning.

Another conspiracy theory intersected with the Fowler/chemical weapons scenario. In the early 1970s, Catherine Dalton, the widow of the Deputy Chief Scientist of the Australian Atomic Energy Commission, Clifford Dalton, published a book, *Without Hardware*, in which she claimed that her New Zealand–born husband had been murdered for helping the Dutch break the American monopoly on nuclear-enriched fuel. Giving the story credibility was Dr Dalton's reputation as the inventor of the fast-breeder nuclear reactor. Catherine Dalton attributed her husband's death from cancer 'to poisoning by malevolent elements of the intelligence community'.[41]

She went on to claim that Gilbert Bogle was Dr Dalton's closest friend, who was helping her investigate his death when he too was murdered, along with Mrs Chandler.

In her book, Mrs Dalton claimed evil forces were at work within Australian science, intelligence agencies, government and even the public service. Newspaper headlines declared confidently: 'Political Assassination' and 'Bogle Died Because He Knew Too Much'. But people named in the book criticised it as a mishmash of speculation and unsubstantiated claims by a deranged woman.

As a young filmmaker in the early 1980s, I was interested in adapting her story into a feature film. I telephoned her and she agreed to come to Sydney and for me to pick her up at Central Railway station. As we walked to my car, Catherine nervously looked behind her. She said that during the production of her book, the printing presses were smashed and threats were made against her life. She claimed she applied for and received 'the protection of the Queen' but only within Commonwealth territory, such as Canberra. In Sydney, she said she had no protection from those who wished her harm. I was taken aback when Catherine got into the back seat, laid down and demanded I drive at no more than 30 kilometres per hour to a large interstate bus station; a crowded venue, where she said we could have privacy!

Over bad coffee and stale cake, she told me how she hand-delivered copies of her book to every Senator in the Federal Parliament. In early 1972, South Australian Labor Senator James Cavanagh took up her cause, quizzing the Government as to whether:

> Bogle's death was a matter for discussion at a specifically convened meeting of Federal Cabinet in March 1963?
>
> The Attorney General had also discussed Bogle with several leading members of the Federal Government and a leading member of the judiciary?
>
> The Federal Government had given a directive to all State police forces that the interest of national security

> could best be served by the police not discovering who was responsible for Bogle's death?

The Secretary of the Cabinet Office, John Bunting, prepared a response to the questions. He said there was no specially convened meeting of the Federal Cabinet in March 1963 to discuss the Bogle case. Furthermore, Cabinet records revealed that the Bogle matter had not been discussed between the deaths and the Coronial Inquest.

But Senator Cavanagh had more questions of the Government. Fighting interjectors, he added that Geoffrey Chandler had received numerous phone calls over six months from an anonymous person telling him things about the case. The caller did not identify himself because he said he was in fear for his life. These claims, the Senator said, were in line with allegations made by Catherine Dalton in her book:

> It is claimed that Dr Bogle, because of his scientific activities and his transfer to America, became a danger to American operations in Australia, and his killing was a justified killing.

One could read this sentence many times and still not make sense of it. Bogle was going to America to work for a respected American firm. Why would American agents in Australia, if they did exist, decide that his working for an American firm was against American interests? Would it not have been simpler to ban his entry into America as they had done with other

Australian scientists, including the famous nuclear pioneer, Sir Mark Oliphant?

Senator Cavanagh presented a bizarre question to the senator representing the Attorney General:

> Did the Australian Security Intelligence Organisation (ASIO) assist an Australian citizen and a central European diplomat to leave Australia within 24 hours of the discovery of the bodies of Dr Bogle and Mrs Chandler at Lane Cove? If so, would a description of the diplomat resemble the description given in evidence at the subsequent Inquest of a man seen running from Lane Cove?

As well as professing knowledge of the Bogle affair, Cavanagh said Mrs Dalton had warned officials in advance about the disappearance of Harold Holt and an assassination attempt on Opposition leader Arthur Calwell. Cavanagh demanded answers from the bemused government senators opposite, but received none.

On reviewing Dalton's book, Police Commissioner Allan was scathing: 'Rambling rubbish. It is worthless—just jumbled jargon. I am satisfied there is not one thing in it that would justify its further investigation.'

Mrs Dalton's self-published manuscript remains a milestone in Australian publishing history, if for no other reason than for the free publicity it received courtesy of the Federal Senate.

◆ ◆ ◆

In the early 1980s, the *National Times* newspaper, which based its reputation on investigative journalism, discovered that the FBI had an 18-page Top Secret file on Dr Bogle. Suspicions were raised when the FBI denied the paper access to the file. 'Could its contents answer Australia's greatest unsolved crime?' the paper asked.

In October 1984, the *National Times* offered yet another revelation:

> According to excellent sources from that organisation, ASIO was conducting an undercover operation affecting Bogle and his associates just before the murders. The details are still secret. But these sources say the undercover activities may help explain why the FBI has 18 pages of documents on the case, which it is still withholding in their entirety.

The article offered no more detail, but by placing ASIO and the FBI together the *National Times* had hashed together a conspiracy of silence, which many people believed.

As it was, the New South Wales Police knew exactly what was in the FBI file. During the original investigation, Police Commissioner Allan wrote to law enforcement agencies around the world asking whether they had ever had a similar case.

On 11 February 1963, six weeks after the deaths, one such letter was sent directly to FBI Director, J. Edgar

Hoover, requesting the FBI's assistance in solving the mystery. It comprised a two-page covering letter and six attachments—totalling twelve pages—relating to police and scientific investigations. Hoover's response, which was negative, comprises the remaining four pages of the 18-page dossier. If Bogle had questioned a driving offence by electing to take it to court, the subsequent police file would have easily exceeded 18 pages.

In reality, Bogle was not going to work on Top Secret projects at Bell Laboratories. Throughout his career he had deliberately chosen not to work on defence-related projects.

Bogle's research colleague Doug Milne argues that there was nothing about his work on Masers that could have made him the target of a foreign power:

> The Maser amplifier that we were working on was a very sensitive radio receiver to pick up signals from distant galaxies and quasars of radio astronomy objects, sources of radio signals. It was not a death ray or anything like that. In fact the maser that we were working on was not even like a laser. It didn't transmit signals. It received signals. The workings of the maser were well publicised, published over many years in engineering journals, scientific journals. I don't think there were any real secrets left in building masers.

In 1984, former top British intelligence officer Peter Wright claimed in Sydney's *Daily Mirror* that Dr Bogle was eliminated after he became a Russian agent working inside Australia's security service, ASIO.[42]

FBI Director, J. Edgar Hoover

Wright alleged that senior MI5 officer Roger Hollis, who was to become MI5's Director General, had recommended ASIO take on Bogle as an agent in 1949 when Hollis came to Australia.

Wright made his extraordinary claim while writing his controversial book, *Spycatcher*, which alleged Hollis was a Russian mole. Therefore by deduction, Bogle too was suspect.

The problem with Wright's story is that Bogle was not living in Australia in 1949. He didn't arrive here until 1957. Moreover, if Wright had evidence that Bogle was a double agent and was assassinated by MI5—perhaps the gravest allegation an intelligence officer could make about his own agency—one would think he would have put the claim in his book. When the tome finally appeared the following year, there was no mention of Dr Bogle at all.

Wright was one of dozens of conspiracy theorists fighting for oxygen. But none provided hard or logical evidence to demonstrate how or why Dr Bogle and Mrs Chandler were 'assassinated' on the bank of the Lane Cove River.

11th February, 1963.

J. Edgar Hoover, Esq.,
Director, Federal Bureau of Investigation,
U.S. Department of Justice,
Washington, 25. D.C.
UNITED STATES OF AMERICA.

CONFIDENTIAL.

Dear Sir,

This Department is investigating the deaths of Dr. Gilbert Stanley Bogle and Mrs. Margaret Olive Chandler whose bodies were found on a river bank near Fullers Bridge, Lane Cove, Sydney, on the morning of the 1st January, 1963.

Since that date intensive inquiries have been conducted by this Department's Criminal Investigation Branch, and the circumstances surrounding the discovery of the bodies together with the result of pertinent aspects of the investigations to date are summarised in the attached photostat marked "A".

The post mortem examinati n of the bodies was conducted by the Director of the Division of Forensic Medicine, Sydney, and his assistant. I have obtained from the Director reports of the autopsies and I attach photostat copies of the reports which are marked "B".

Specimens from the lungs, heart, kidneys, brains, livers, bowels and blood of the deceased were submitted to pathological examination, the result of which is set out in the photostat marked "C".

Toxicological Investigation of the stomachs and contents, the intestines, livers, kidneys, spleens and blood was made by the Government Analyst and the result of his investigations is contained in the photostat marked "D".

"Radiation" examinations were made of the bodies and the result is set out in the photostat marked "E".

In addition, the assistance of the Professor of Pharmacology of the University of Sydney was sought and he has reported the result of his investigations - see photostat marked "F".

Despite the foregoing scientific and medico-legal investigations it has not been possible to determine the cause of death and as you might well imagine, great public interest has been taken not only in this State, but in the whole of the Commonwealth of Australia, in the cases.

I have conferred with the Director of Forensic Medicine, the Government Analyst and the Professor of Pharmacology and told them that I propose to seek your aid in advising whether there is any record in your Department of death having occurred in similar circumstances where the difficulties experienced here in determining the cause were also encountered. It is agreed by these Officers that such information, if available, could be of assistance to them.

I would now ask......

16. The Watcher

In late February 1963, some eight weeks after the deaths of Dr Bogle and Mrs Chandler, the NSW Police contacted their federal counterparts for assistance. They wanted to know if Geoffrey Chandler had ever been involved in defence research.

The Commonwealth Police sent Sergeant A.G. Tilton to meet with Colonel Graham, the Director of Military Intelligence. Tilton asked whether Geoffrey Chandler had ever been engaged in defence work at the Standard Laboratories in Melbourne. If so, he said, 'all possible information was required concerning his work or studies, in particular, that concerning chemical warfare or development of any viruses'.

Colonel Graham promised immediate action. That same day, Sergeant Tilton called on a Mr Edmunds at the Federal Attorney General's Department also to discuss Geoffrey Chandler and a possible chemical weapons connection.[43]

The intriguing aspect of this inquiry was that Australia was not officially undertaking either chemical or biological warfare research in the 1960s. In the end, joint Commonwealth Police–Military Intelligence investigation found no evidence to connect Geoffrey

Chandler with the mysterious Melbourne laboratory or chemical weapons research.

It makes sense that the police wanted to know everything they could about Chandler. He was the most likely suspect, after all. While Military Intelligence and the Commonwealth Police were happy to cooperate with the investigation, Australia's spy agency, ASIO, took eight years before it revealed its connection with someone under investigation.

In 1971, following Catherine Dalton's allegations, the NSW Government demanded the police ask what ASIO knew about Dr Bogle. Their answer was unexpected and until now has never been made public.

ASIO said it had nothing on Dr Bogle. But it did have an interest in someone else associated with the case—Geoffrey Chandler.

From the outset of the atomic age, scientists were pawns in the business of espionage. Their knowledge was almost as valuable as military intelligence, particularly in the area of weapons and atomic research. Chandler and Bogle's employer, the CSIRO, was itself a product of espionage fears. In 1947, United States and British spy agencies became concerned that its predecessor, CSIR, employed communists, some of whom were allegedly aiding the Soviet Union. Indeed, about a dozen CSIR scientists were members of the Communist Party of Australia and at least one was known to be in contact with Soviet officials.

A crisis emerged in 1948 when America stopped passing classified information to Australia. The ban threatened defence cooperation not only with

Washington but also with London and put at risk the Top Secret British/Australian missile project at Woomera, in South Australia.

British Prime Minister Clement Attlee and the head of MI5, Sir Percy Sillitoe, convinced the Australian Prime Minister, Ben Chifley, to set up an intelligence agency along the lines of MI5 to 'ensure the security of the Empire'.[44] Chifley also agreed to make 'reasonable adjustments in the constitution of the scientific organisations serving the Australian Government.'[45] The following year, the CSIR was replaced by the CSIRO and its employees were to be vetted by the new security agency, ASIO.

Theoretically, if ASIO held suspicions about any applicant for a position with the CSIRO being a communist, he or she would have been denied employment.

In the early 1950s, well before joining CSIRO, Chandler had worked with electronics firms AWA and EMI. During his tenure at EMI, Chandler underwent ASIO vetting:

> I was working for EMI on transponders for a Long-range Weapon establishment in South Australia. They were firing their rockets down the range and they had transponders to send back data during the course of the flight of the rocket. I was involved with the very early stages of integrated circuit design and construction, so I had to have a security clearance for that. I was just a junior technical assistant, but you had to be classified. So ASIO had investigated me and found that I was pure

> white and 21, and satisfactory to work on long range weapons classified material. So the answer should have been, 'he's clean'.

When Chandler applied to join CSIRO, ASIO provided further clearance. But Geoffrey's acquaintances in the Push had an uneasy feeling about him. In her book *Sex and Anarchy*, Anne Coombs suggests it was a common suspicion within the Push that Geoffrey Chandler was a 'watcher':

> Chandler was known as someone who hung around. Some people found him a little strange, somewhat closed off, watchful. Later, when his wife's death had brought him notoriety, there was even speculation that he might have been an ASIO plant.

As it turns out, those suspicions were well founded. While ASIO said it had no interest in Dr Bogle, it admitted that Geoffrey Chandler was an informer.

In 2006, I interviewed Geoffrey Chandler on camera and asked if he had ever been an ASIO agent. Chandler immediately went silent. He asked to have the camera turned off and said he needed to go to the bathroom. I assumed that was the end of the interview. Ten minutes later he returned to the studio and said, 'roll camera'. He then proceeded to tell me about how a couple of ASIO officers came to see him:

> ASIO asked me questions about this person and that person. They asked me questions about my associates—

> what I did with them and so on. What were my views, what were their views? Because they were pretty toey about things in those days when you were in a sensitive area. I suppose it was sort of cross-character referencing. No doubt they probably asked somebody that knew me, about me. So in that sense I suppose you could say that I worked for them, but specifically as a sort of paid job, no.

In 1971, ASIO told the police that Chandler was an informant embedded inside the Communist Party of Australia. After working with EMI, Chandler had moved to the Department of Civil Aviation, then to a private company as assistant to the chief engineer. But the recession of 1952 had landed Chandler on the dole. It was then that he flirted with communism:

> There were mass strikes and a big recession, and lots and lots of people out of work. So I had no hesitation whatsoever in joining them.

Despite his connections with the Communist Party of Australia (CPA), Chandler received ASIO clearance to work for the CSIRO. On the surface, this defies logic, since communists were strictly forbidden from employment with the science body. Unless, of course, he had been 'turned'. This may have come in the form of a simple inducement: 'We know you are a communist. Help us by becoming an informant and you keep your job.'

Former leading Communist Party member Bob Gould believed that Chandler was a very active agent.

Gould's own massive declassified ASIO file contains references to Geoffrey Chandler. On one occasion, surveillance officers picked up the two men walking along a city street together.

Gould alleged Chandler encouraged CPA meetings to be held in his home. It wasn't until Chandler rented his residence to a visiting British Socialist that his motives were discovered. An intermittent overhead light resulted in the visitor calling an electrician. Within the ceiling, the electrician allegedly found that every room in the house was bugged. According to Gould, from that point on Chandler was persona non-grata within the Communist Party.

I called Geoffrey Chandler to comment on Gould's allegation. He said he could not recall holding CPA meetings at his home and denied any knowledge of his house being bugged, though he did admit informing on the CPA.

Geoffrey Chandler believed that his ASIO connections did have an impact on the Bogle-Chandler case. Within days of the deaths of his wife and Dr Bogle, prominent Sydney barrister, Kevin Murray, approached him:

> He made an appointment to see me out of the blue. We met at the Forest Lodge Hotel after work and he said something like, 'There's going to be an Inquest. Do you have any representation?' He said, 'Unless you are represented you are going to be churned up into mince meat.' I said, 'No, it never occurred to me that I would require a representative.' My attitude was that only guilty

people required representation and I wasn't guilty so why should I require representation? But being a little bit more worldly-wise he pointed out the error of that view and offered his services for free. So I accepted. Then, of course, later one wonders why Kevin Murray turned up and offered his services. Was he really being altruistic or was there sinister motivation behind his generosity?

Chandler and his lawyer, Kevin Murray

Kevin Murray, who was building a reputation as a criminal lawyer, had a military establishment background. He was a Lieutenant Colonel in the Sydney University Regiment—one of the oldest infantry regiments in the Australian Army. In 1971, despite keeping many of Sydney's most high-profile crooks out of prison, he was made an Officer of the Order of the

British Empire. In his reflective years, Chandler began to suspect Murray was under instructions from ASIO:

> I think it is highly likely and highly probable that Murray was acting on instructions from higher up and he was designed or intended, directed to keep this and that out of the newspapers or from public presentation. That's quite feasible. And after all he was a good barrister and he probably got paid quite well for doing all this for free for me.

As it turned out, Chandler's secret association with ASIO was never revealed. One can only imagine the sensation this information would have caused had the media got wind of it at the height of the investigation.

17. Acid Test

While many theories were not taken seriously, some were investigated and reinvestigated. High on that list was an overdose of the drug LSD. Journalist Gerald Stone:

> Under what kind of circumstances could you think of two people being poisoned? It's hard to make a person take a poison pill. So what was it? The poison was never identified. So then came the speculation. We knew that there were strange drugs like LSD that people took to give them psychedelic trips and so on. And the assumption was that maybe somebody, as a trick even, or as an encouragement, had put LSD in both of their drinks to send them off to have a good time.

LSD—lysergic acid diethylamide—was first synthesised in 1938 by chemist Dr Albert Hofmann of Sandoz Laboratories in Switzerland. Originally developed as a possible circulatory and respiratory stimulant, the drug eventually gained popularity in the 1950s as a research tool in studies of mental illnesses, including schizophrenia, alcoholism, criminal behaviour and sexual perversions, including homosexuality.[46]

In the early 1950's, the CIA began experimenting with LSD on unwitting US citizens as a possible truth drug. Hundreds of participants, including CIA agents, military personnel, prostitutes, and mental patients, were given LSD—many without their knowledge or consent. Some experiments were nothing less than severe psychological torture. A number of victims committed suicide, while others wound up in psychiatric wards. In the end, the CIA researchers realised that LSD's effects were too varied and uncontrollable to make it of any practical use as a truth drug.[47]

In the late 1950s, both Aldous Huxley of *Brave New World* fame and 'Beat' poet, Allen Ginsberg, experimented with the drug. But it was Harvard psychology professor Timothy Leary who, in 1960, heralded LSD in the mainstream media. Later dubbed by President Richard Nixon as 'the most dangerous man in America', Leary told *Playboy* magazine that LSD was a powerful aphrodisiac. Concerns about its safety, led to its being outlawed in the United States in 1962. Predictably, prohibition created a black market and an explosion in the use of LSD, especially among students and intellectuals.[48]

LSD was being imported into Australia in 1962, but it was in limited recreational use and largely restricted to those with connections to the scientific and medical communities. Detectives considered the Psychiatry Department of the University of Sydney as a possible source of the drug. The laboratories of Dr Bogle and Geoffrey Chandler were also located within the Sydney University campus. Therefore, they deduced, the potential of either man coming into contact with the drug was certainly higher than for the rest of society. Moreover, Pamela Logan, Geoffrey Chandler's lover, was a secretary in the Psychiatry Department.

I contacted a former researcher in the Psychiatry Department who told me that there was no research into LSD at Sydney University at the time and it was not until years later that it really became part of the campus scene amongst students. There was some suggestion that Bogle might have manufactured the drug himself. Scientific detectives went to his laboratory and took away ten bottles of chemicals from his lab. None of the chemicals were the precursors required for LSD production.

In a recent interview Geoffrey Chandler offered this perspective:

> As far as I'm aware, at that period of Sydney's history, LSD wasn't terribly readily available. I had no knowledge of LSD at that time and wouldn't have known it if I had fallen over it. Ten years later there was plenty of it around everywhere, but not as far as I was aware [in 1962]. I don't think Margaret would have taken anything willingly, anything of that sort of nature.

The question is, can LSD kill?

Compared with other hallucinogenic substances, LSD is one hundred times more potent than psilocybin or 'magic mushrooms' and 4,000 times more potent than mescaline. The dosage level inducing a hallucinogenic effect in humans is miniscule, averaging only 25 micrograms or about one-tenth the mass of the smallest grain of sand.

While LSD was a product of professional chemists, it was anything but scientifically meted out. In the early 1960s, its distribution was mostly as small doses on squares of blotting paper. A number of hallucinating users had reportedly died from misadventure, such as jumping out of windows or in front of vehicles while drugged. In November 1953, US Army biochemist Frank Olsen committed suicide after taking the drug in a classified CIA experiment. And while it was generally assumed a person could die from an overdose of LSD, there were no reported cases anywhere in the world in 1963.

In *Psychosomatic Medicine: Principles and Practice* the authors state: 'LSD has a large "therapeutic index" and no human deaths have been reported with LSD overdose alone.'[49]

Joseph Newman claimed in *What Everyone Needs To Know About Drugs*: 'No deaths have been directly attributed to the drug's impact on the body.'

A death from an LSD overdose did occur in Britain in the late 1980s. During a prison visit, a woman transferred a massive quantity of the drug to a prisoner's mouth via a kiss. The luckless man swallowed the illicit substance and died a terrible death. The quantity was estimated to be about 400 times the normal dosage.

Newspapermen continued to perpetuate the theory that LSD was the cause of death in the Bogle-Chandler case. Bill Jenkings from the *Daily Mirror* claimed that a number of other guests at the Nash party 'were frequent users of LSD'. He gave no proof and there was nothing in the police case files to substantiate such a claim.

Twelve months after the deaths, the rumours persisted, accompanied by claims that Sydney was awash with the drug and there were wild parties at several psychiatric hospitals. The Minister for Health denied the veracity of the rumours. The Police Commissioner, Norman Allan, told the *Sydney Morning Herald* that LSD as a suspect poison had been discarded months earlier following intensive police, medical and scientific investigations.

Indeed, a few days after the deaths of Bogle and Chandler, the Government Analyst, Samuel Ogg, asked his chief toxicologist, Vivian Mahoney, to test for LSD. Mahoney's attitude was to keep an open mind. The police provided a sample of the drug to do a comparative analysis, but Mahoney found no LSD in the tissue samples of either victims.

Detective Ron Rudgley verified that tests were carried out:

> LSD was one of the drugs that were considered as the possible cause but like all the rest we had nothing to substantiate that LSD was the cause of the deaths.

Three decades later, however, LSD was again in the news as the suspect poison that killed Bogle and Chandler. In late 1995, the head of the New South Wales Institute of Forensic Medicine, Dr Jo Duflou, attended an international conference in Europe and met Frederic Rieders, a renowned American forensic toxicologist. Rieders quizzed him about the famous Bogle-Chandler case and speculation about LSD as the cause of death. Rieders convinced Duflou that if LSD was present, he had the equipment to find it.

Dr Duflou returned to Sydney and found some relic tissue samples, possibly left over from Professor Thorp's analysis, which he despatched to Rieders' Pennsylvania laboratory. In January 1996, Sydney newspapers proclaimed the mystery solved. Evidence of LSD had been found in the tissues of Dr Bogle! But when Duflou attempted to contact Rieders to obtain the results of a more sensitive testing, the toxicologist would not take his call or return his messages. When Duflou finally did speak with Rieders, he learnt that the second screening had proven negative.

To Dr Duflou's chagrin the media was not interested in correcting the story.

Even though there was never any evidence to prove that the victims had used LSD, many Australians, including surviving detectives of the era, still believe LSD to be the cause of the deaths of Dr Bogle and Mrs Chandler.

18. Sole Witness

Lane Cove River

In November 2004, I began researching the Bogle-Chandler case for a television documentary. My interest was in exploring its impact on the media, policing and Sydney society. I had no ambition to find a solution to the crime. In retrospect, there was little reason for any broadcaster to back the film. But having grown up near the Lane Cove River and having long been intrigued by the Bogle-Chandler mystery, it was a story that I was itching to research in depth.

One afternoon in October 2004 I posted a letter to the NSW Police, requesting access to the case files. On my return from the post office, I took a nap. As I dozed off, I realised there was little motivation for the police to cooperate. About 20 minutes later, I awoke with a thought. There had been a 'witness' to the deaths of Dr Bogle and Mrs Chandler that I was certain had not been investigated—the river itself.

Over the previous 20 years, I had read almost everything in the public domain about the case, but there had been no mention of the most obvious feature of the 'crime scene'—the mangroves, which line the Lane Cove River from its mouth at Figtree to the weir, just past Fullers Bridge. Recalling my schoolboy science, I knew that mangroves produce gases, including hydrogen sulphide (H_2S), a colourless gas that reeks of rotten eggs. I knew the noxious odour well from our school science laboratory when a budding chemist in the class was carted off to hospital by ambulance after illicitly manufacturing the gas as a practical joke. As it turned out, the boy was very lucky not to have died; in high concentrations, H_2S is as deadly as hydrogen cyanide—the gas used by governments and executioners to rid their societies of their least favourite criminals.

Researching the gas afresh, I discovered that hydrogen sulphide poisoning is a common cause of death in sewers, farms and industrial situations, such as oil refineries. And it has its own individual, somewhat sinister, killing characteristics. Like most gases, it is most dangerous in confined spaces. But because it is heavier than air, hydrogen sulphide will linger in open spaces close to the ground if the air is cool and still.

The human nose can detect hydrogen sulphide at low concentrations, starting below one part per million (ppm). But between 100 and 150ppm, the gas overcomes the olfactory nerve in the nose and we are oblivious to its presence. According to health and safety experts, this is when the gas becomes extremely dangerous. Between 300 and 500ppm fluid builds up in the lungs and the victim suffers dizziness, excitement, staggering gait and diarrhoea. Between 700 and 800ppm the gas paralyses the respiratory centre, leading to rapid unconsciousness and death.

Mangroves

At levels of 800 to 1,000ppm hydrogen sulphide is lethal. Most fatalities occur after only one or two breaths—the so-called 'slaughterhouse sledge-hammer effect'.

Hydrogen sulphide kills by interfering with the brain's respiratory command centre, which sends nerve signals to the lungs. Death after a single exposure to high concentrations appears to be the result of respiratory failure or cardiac arrest, with most victims presenting with respiratory insufficiency, non-cardiogenic pulmonary oedema, coma, and cyanosis—the same symptoms experienced by Bogle and Chandler.

The day after posting my letter to the police, I drove to the Lane Cove River and retraced Bogle and Chandler's steps down the bush track to where their bodies were found. The scene was peaceful and still, the river brown-green in colour and barely flowing. Full-grown mangrove trees lined the waterway. Using descriptions from a number of published sources, I located roughly where Bogle's body was found on the edge of the riverbank. Margaret Chandler's body was reportedly found about 15 metres further south on the riverbed, itself.

Reaching out of the rich brown mud, like dead men's fingers, were the mangroves' breathing apparatus, the pneumatophores. A sweet smell of rotting leaves and eucalyptus hung in the air, but there was no odour of rotten eggs—the signature feature of hydrogen sulphide. I wondered whether mangroves could give off enough hydrogen sulphide to be fatal. Surely millions of people throughout history have ventured into mangroves and suffered no ill effect.

I wrote to Dr Jes Sammut at the University of NSW. Without mentioning the Bogle-Chandler case, I asked whether if someone was found dead in a mangrove area, could H_2S have caused the death? His response was tantalising:

> Hydrogen sulphide can be gassed off from mangroves and other swamps, but I am not sure if it can at sufficient quantities to kill. I recall doing fieldwork on acid sulphate soils in Tuckean Swamp in northern NSW and feeling ill from the smell of hydrogen sulphide gas coming out of the anaerobic sediments of the swamp. I was in a closed forest so the gas, which is heavier than air, was sitting low to the ground. I could smell it but the problem with the gas is that you can quickly stop smelling it. I don't know of any fatalities from it in mangroves, though. It could possibly occur if there is no wind to move it around. There are many factors to consider—the pH of the soil and water, position of the water table, air movement and depressions in the landscape.

For a second opinion, Dr Sammut suggested I contact Professor Ian White at the Australian National University. His response was equally intriguing:

> There is no question that hydrogen sulphide (H_2S) is produced in mangrove swamps. Often it reacts with soluble iron to form harmless iron sulphides. H_2S is fairly quickly oxidised to sulphur dioxide (SO2) in the presence of sunlight. We have found coming from mangrove swamp-type soils that SO2 is given off during the day but H_2S is given off at night. Since the reduction of sulphate to H_2S is a bacterially catalysed reaction, it

> is temperature dependent: the warmer the conditions, the faster the rate of H_2S evolution. If the location was stagnant, if it was early in the morning in summer and the victim was in a depression, then it is certainly possible that the cause of death was H_2S poisoning.

Professor White added that deaths had occurred in mangroves on a Pacific atoll. Two men digging a sewer line to a depth of three to four metres had disturbed a pocket of gas and were asphyxiated.

There were a number of aspects to both opinions that fitted the Bogle-Chandler case, particularly the time of day and the proximity to the ground. But I was not convinced that in normal circumstances mangroves were killers, even if one was to lie down at water level at dawn. I wondered whether increased levels of the gas were being emitted from the Lane Cove River mangroves in the early 1960s.

I contacted environmental historian Lynne McLoughlin. Her insights into the river's environmental past were invaluable:

> For over the 200 years of settlement, the Lane Cove River was a major arterial corridor and the main way people got in and out of the area, both for industry and produce. It was a major form of transport for the timber first and then for the produce from the orchards; citrus, pears, apples and peaches had to get to markets and the river was used quite a lot. Industries set up along the river again because of the transport.[50]

Intriguingly, at the time of European settlement in 1788 there were no mangroves on the river.

> With the clearing of the steep slopes, lots of sediment ran into the river and silted it up and gave mangroves an opportunity to develop. In addition, in the 1920s a sewer line was placed all the way down the river. This was an enormous disturbance. The building methods were hardly very environmentally sensitive and the river has paid the price ever since. So these kinds of things that happened over 200 years encouraged the spread of mangroves.

Despite these dramatic changes to the waterway, McLoughlin said it remained one of the most beautiful in the Sydney Basin. Its close proximity to the city and transport made it a haven for Sydneysiders on weekends and holidays:

> The most delightful use of the river from the turn of the century, 1900, through to about the war, was as a major site for picnicking. People would catch the ferry at Circular Quay and travel up to Hunters Hill where the ferry terminated and then they'd get out there and they'd hire rowboats and row up the river. And the stories and accounts from the period of the state of the river at that time are just wonderful. They talked about it as a veritable fairyland. People would get out of their rowboats and gather wildflowers from the shore. There were people who made a living along the river from selling strawberries and cream or hot water to the picnickers, as they came along.

In the 1920s and 1930s the most popular destination on the river was the Fairyland Pleasure Grounds; a delightful, aptly named reserve where hundreds of picnickers whiled away the day on rugs, in rowing boats or playing ball games. Fairyland even boasted a dance hall.

Fairyland

But in the late 1930s, about the time a weir was constructed at Fullers Bridge, visitors started to abandon the lower half of the river for recreation. Local residents, whose houses backed onto the river, began to complain of strange illnesses, nausea, shortness of breath and that the paint was peeling from their roofs and their taps were blackening. There was also an objectionable odour engulfing the entire neighbourhood.

McLoughlin directed me to the Lane Cove Library, where I discovered the extraordinary extent of the problem in a file containing correspondence between riverside residents and the Council. For six months, from May to October 1939, the residents complained that the river was discoloured and smelt of 'rotten eggs'.

In July 1941, another local resident wrote of another serious pollution event on the river. Green weed was in abundance and fish and eels were destroyed. The stench, he said, lasted several months. Another resident observed that an 'abnormal smell emanates from the river during the small hours of the morning'.

Correspondence in the Council file revealed that the odour reappeared year after year and lingered for months at a time.

The letters were unexpected, but exactly what I was looking for. Here was evidence that there was far more hydrogen sulphide than one would find being emitted from a normal mangrove environment.

In September 1947, the *Sun* newspaper reported on a major catastrophic event:

> A heavy smell of rotten eggs has been hanging over the district for weeks. The Ryde Town Clerk said today that he had driven over the bridge and the smell was 'something awful'. One resident interviewed today said, 'The water is sometimes full of bodies of dead bream, mullet and eels. Bream are not usually found this high up-river. They apparently swim ahead of the muck trying to escape it, but are finally caught in it and killed just below the weir.

Two months later, in November 1947, the putrid stench was still blanketing the neighbourhood and the gas was further impacting on human health. A local resident wrote to Council complaining that overpowering fumes from the river had caused vomiting.

In February 1949 another local complained to Council:

> The gas was so offensive and comprised so large a part of the atmosphere that breathing was difficult and almost painful. Although the ratepayer may be prepared to suffer if the paintwork of his house is damaged, he is likely to take unusually strong action if he is forced to witness his child's gasping for breath.[51]

A transport and town planning inquiry into the state of Sydney's rivers backed the residents' complaints:

> The upper reaches [of the Lane Cove River] above Fig Tree Bridge are badly silted and choked with weeds, even fish are dying and a most offensive odour is given off. Some improvement was made when the Lane Cove National Park was constructed but the section between there and Fig Tree Bridge has been allowed to deteriorate to a deplorable extent.[52]

Meanwhile, the Lane Cove Council's Chief Health Inspector responded to complaints from residents who lived directly opposite the location where Bogle and Chandler would later die:

> Inspections were made of the banks and interviews were held with occupiers of dwellings in the vicinity of

Fullers Bridge

> Fullers Bridge. On the first occasion, the river was at half tide, some small dead fish were lying on the bank and at the edge of the water and an unbearable foul smell permeated the air in the immediate vicinity and was noticeable for some distance away from the river. The water was discoloured (inclined to be milky grey) and the mud at and near height watermark was black and when disturbed most objectionable.[53]

The Health Inspector could not identify the cause of the problem but suggested rotting algae, industrial waste, or a combination of the two was to blame. Finally, after ten years of complaints, the Lane Cove Town Clerk wrote to the New South Wales State Government: 'The stench is causing sickness amongst the residents on the riverfront and is reported to be affecting external paintwork and internal house fittings.'

The Town Clerk also complained to the Secretary, Maritime Services Board:

> Unless some solution to the trouble can be found and remedial measures taken, a valuable residential section of the Municipality will be absolutely ruined.[54]

Between 1941 and 1947 there had been 13 major pollution episodes. The problem was now so serious that the Council suggested the entire residential area beside the river might have to be evacuated.

With the issue now a political one, the Maritime Services Board dispatched their leading marine scientist to the river to investigate.

Despite the passage of almost 60 years, I was able to track down the scientist. In his 80s and confined to a wheelchair, Maurice Fry clearly remembered his investigation of the Lane Cove River.

As we settled down to talk, he asked if my father had ever worked for the Maritime Services Board. I said he had and told him my father's Christian name. Fry smiled and said they had worked together. Occasionally, my father had captained Fry's boat on scientific surveys of Sydney's waterways, including the Lane Cove River. It seemed an astonishing coincidence.

Fry recalled that his investigation of the river took a year to complete. Every few weeks, he would charter a small open launch to collect samples. On his first survey trip, he was in no doubt about the identity of odour coming from the river:

> It was very nauseating and I didn't feel too good when I was actually working on the river because the concentration of hydrogen sulphide was quite high. We

> were in a boat, but one would not have chosen to be out on there, it was only a matter of necessity. We carried out our work as quickly as possible and got out of the place. I would say that it would have been the most polluted river at the time.[55]

Fry established testing points along the waterway where measurements would be taken regularly throughout the year. Fry found that low oxygen levels coincided with excessive hydrogen sulphide production. However, the source of the gas was not the mangroves. The entire riverbed of the tidal section of the river from Fullers Bridge to its mouth—a distance of five kilometres—was saturated with hydrogen sulphide to a maximum depth of half a metre.

The result was something that Fry had never witnessed before:

> Finally, the hydrogen sulphide pressure reached such intensity that the bottom virtually exploded. When this occurred the surface waters became rapidly black, due to suspension of black mud particles as well as iron sulphide. The excessive un-oxidised hydrogen sulphide escaped to the atmosphere in large quantities and nauseated the neighbourhood, and the gas in the water poisoned fish and other biological life.

During his time on the river, Maurice Fry witnessed the toll of another major pollution event, which left the waterway black and putrid:

> Every few yards there was a large fish, big ones and little ones, but mainly they seemed to be large. They were lining the banks at inter-tidal level. And the eels, they were remarkable; they were all up at the weir, trying to jump up over the weir into the fresh water. According to the Council, truckloads of fish were taken away.

Mud samples revealed that the river bottom was carpeted with decaying red-coloured microorganisms called Glenodium. These disturbed the natural balance in the mud, causing a dominance of hydrogen sulphide producing saprophytic bacteria, which live on dead organic matter. The hydrogen sulphide in the water poisoned fish and other life, which then started to putrefy. Some of the gas was oxidised to sulphate, colouring the water white, while the rest escaped into the atmosphere, nauseating the neighbourhood.[56]

Fry's next priority was to identify the source of

the problem. The culprit he believed had to be one or more of the factories, which lined the river. Industries, including a vinegar producer, a chemical company and two tanning factories had used Sydney's most beautiful river and its tributaries as a virtual sewer for their waste. In his report, Fry noted:

Maurice Fry

> Offensive residue from the [tannery's] de-hairing plant—composed of hair, small particles of flesh—is collected in settlement pits from which it is allowed to overflow and discharge into the river near the head of Burns Bay.[57]

Around the same time, a health inspector found that waste from one of the tanning factories appeared to be killing the mangrove trees. Incredibly, mangroves, which are adapted to hydrogen sulphide-rich environments, could not survive such toxicity.

Records show that the Lane Cove River had long been seen as a legitimate location to dispose of industrial waste. In 1883, a bone dust manufacturer operated a boiling down works on the river. The owner John Berry gave evidence at a Royal Commission into Noxious Trades about his new works:

> 'How do you dispose of the waste fluids?'
>
> 'They run into the river—into the Lane Cove River.'
>
> 'Is that the method apt to lodge anything on the shore?'
>
> 'No; there is such a current that 20 yards (18 metres) from the building there is nothing to see, either up or down; there is a strong tide just there.'
>
> 'Then, without that river, and with no sewer to carry off this waste fluid, you would not know how to dispose of it?'
>
> 'If I had no river and no sewer it would have to do as it does in many other places—find the best hole it can and get into it.'
>
> 'If your premises were thoroughly drained and all the waste fluids carried away as soon as they are formed, there would be no smell, or not much, about the place, would there?'
>
> 'There is nothing that beats the river...'[58]

In 1894, Berry's bone dust works were forced out of business. Their riverside location was taken over by the Chicago Cornflour and Starch Mills. Owned by Clifford

River Pollution a Worry To Homes

Serious pollution of Lane Cove River, in the tidal part below Fuller's Bridge, has been distressing people living in that area for the past month.

Residents say that the tide brings up a thick blue-black muddy stain in the river, and a heavy smell of rotten eggs has been hanging over the district for weeks.

The Ryde Town Clerk (Mr. F. C. Taylor) said today that he had driven over the bridge several times, and the smell was "something awful."

Vegetable Prices Firm At Markets

Pumpkins were dearer at the City Markets today, prices rising from 14/- to 24/- a cwt.

Other green vegetables sold

Love Pty Limited, the mill's advertising boasted that 'the quality of our cornflour was equal to the best the world can produce'.[59]

But such quality came at a dreadful environmental cost. The mill discharged up to 20 million gallons of sulphurous effluent into the river each year. In 1948, Maurice Fry discovered that the mill was largely responsible for the massive hydrogen sulphide gas in the bottom mud.

Clifford Love chemist Dr Gordon Adkins, who worked at the mill from 1946 to 1955, told me that the company knew it was the source of the river's pollution problem. Dr Adkins said that he and the company scientists were at loggerheads with management about the nasty odours coming from the waterway. He recalled that the galvanised wire clotheslines in the neighbourhood, including his own, corroded because of the hydrogen sulphide gas:

Chicago Mills

> In the factory we burnt sulphur, which was trapped in a special chimney by steamed water droplets, which diluted the sulphur dioxide with the water at about 0.3 per cent strength. This was fed into the grain steeps where corn grain was soaked for some time–to bleach it, soften it and preserve it. The water mix evolved into sulphurous acid, which was totally drained into the Lane Cove River where it became more diluted hydrogen sulphide. This built up in the sediment.[60]

Over its 60 years of operation, the cornflour mill discharged more than five billion litres of sulphuric acid into the river. As a result of Fry's almost forensic investigation, Clifford Love and all the other factories along the waterway were ordered to divert their waste into the sewer. But it was not the total solution. The sewer line, which was one of Sydney's biggest, ran right across the river bottom. Halfway across river, the authorities installed a massive valve. In times of heavy rain, the valve automatically opened, spewing out sewage and industrial waste. After the rain stopped, these 'diversions' would continue for another three days. An average of a billion litres of sewage and industrial waste still ended up in the river each year.

In the 1950s the river's pollution woes continued when three rubbish tips were established in the catchment area. The tips continually seeped putrid runoff into the waterway. But another factor was also in play. Fry believes it was no coincidence that people started to complain about the pollution problems immediately after the weir was built in 1938.

> The weir has aggravated the already precarious dynamic balance in the river by introducing a new set of mechanical and biological factors, and has greatly increased the potentiality of the river to pollution.[61]

By cutting the river in two, the weir severely restricted the tidal flushing and the natural scouring of the river bottom. With the incoming tide, pollutants from the factories were invariably carried upstream by the tide and deposited at or close to the weir.

In April 1951, approximately 5,000,000 mullet and 500,000 eels, weighing in at 9,000 tonnes, gathered near the weir, struggling for the little freshwater still passing through the spillway. Within three weeks, no live fish were to be seen. Tests of the water revealed oxygen levels seriously depleted. A researcher concluded that this lack of oxygen was due to its use in the oxidation of hydrogen sulphide from the sulphur in the mud.

Despite the diversion of industrial waste, hydrogen sulphide events just kept occurring throughout the 1950s and Sydney's *Sun Herald* made it clear where it thought the blame rested:

> Rotten egg gas in the height of summer forces the occupants of nearby houses to close their doors and shutter their windows in gasping confinement. The Lane Cove River weir, which can fairly be regarded as a milestone on the pathway to this particular manifestation of Hell, was constructed to provide an amenity for the National Park there set aside. It actually served to cut off, in its entirety, the trickle of fresh water, which had always flowed into the Harbour at that point. This gave the mussels, the seaweeds and the algae—particularly the algae—a vast new ground in which to establish themselves, an area, which had previously been closed to them because of the brackish water. Seasonally they flourish there in vast quantities, and are seasonally killed by the freshwater when the river floods. The dead algae, giving off sulphuretted hydrogen, poison the fish, and the mussels are killed by the fresh water, and so the menace grows. It happens in March and April, and again in October and November.[62]

In 1966, three years after the Bogle-Chandler tragedy, the upper reaches of the river near the weir were reported to be 'extremely polluted'. Hydrogen sulphide levels were found to be abnormal and oxygen in the river was: 'below minimum levels required to avoid dangerous conditions'.[63]

During 1966, Hunter's Hill High School's Conservation Club carried out tests on water pollution on the river. A *Sydney Morning Herald* reporter joined one of the expeditions:

> Through the mangroves, the mud and the stink, the craft inched onwards. As it grounded the crew leapt overboard sinking almost to their waists in the black stench. The air was tepid, dead. Since the club began earlier this year, several expeditions have set out, and all, miraculously have returned. Some weeks ago, a party of twelve left the river proper and explored the narrow waters of Stringy Bark Creek. Three men materialised and demanded of the boys what they were doing. When told they were taking samples of effluent flowing into the river, there were informed they had no right to be in the creek as it was private property. If they remained, there were in danger of being shot at—presumably with guns.[64]

Despite this wealth of material about the pollution history of the river, it is astonishing that no-one suspected pollutants as a possible cause of the deaths of Bogle and Chandler. There had been scores of complaints from locals about illnesses, vomiting and breathing difficulties, but no one had put two and two together.

Perhaps it was because the average citizen was generally non-scientific and saw smoke-belching, waste-spewing industries as a sign of progress. The Lane Cove River flows into the majestic Parramatta River, the main river feeding into Sydney Harbour. Since European settlement it too has suffered the consequences of industrialisation. In 1947, 9,000 people were employed in 55 industries along a stretch of Parramatta River between the Gladesville Bridge and Parramatta. Most of those industries, which included paint, chemical and battery manufacturers, deposited their liquid waste untreated into the river. Complaints about the river's condition were mainly aimed at removing silt so that larger boats could navigate it and facilitate a 'tremendous industrial expansion'. Occasionally, massive pollution events made it into newspapers. In 1950, the *Sydney Morning Herald* reported on 'thick black sludge' that blanketed 16 kilometres of foreshore along both sides of the river. Parents were forced to use petrol to clean the legs of children who paddled in the river. Concern about the health of the river was generally limited to amateur fishermen. In 1953, a Water Police inspector said:

> Personally, I wouldn't eat a prawn that came out of the Parramatta River. I took home a few we confiscated the other week. Believe me, those prawns tasted of tar. There's the effluent from the factories, the runoff from the roads, the drains—the pollution, in fact.[65]

A few months prior to the deaths of Bogle and Chandler, American scientist Rachel Carson ignited the modern ecological movement with her controversial book *Silent Spring*. Carson told the story of spectacular fish kills in the Colorado River in 1961. Shortly after daylight on Sunday 25 January, dead fish appeared in the Town Lake in Austin and in the river for a distance of about

8 kilometres below the lake. By the next day there were reports of dead fish 80 kilometres downstream. The cause was traced to industrial chemicals that had been pumped into the storm sewer. But Carson was heavily criticised by governments and industry for daring to warn of a connection between pollution and human health.

In Sydney it took until the early 1970s, when the Parramatta River was declared virtually lifeless, for Australia's most populated city to begin to wake up to the fact that pollution had to be curbed. Most fish and other marine life had deserted the oxygen-depleted and dead waters of the upper river. Its tributaries, including the Lane Cove River, were in a similar condition.

The more I investigated the industrial history of the Lane Cove River, the more I believed that chronic pollution could have resulted in the deaths of Gilbert Bogle and Margaret Chandler.

The tipping point was Maurice Fry's scientific report in which he identified the most hazardous section of the Lane Cove River:

> It is interesting to note that the first indication of excessive, as well as the highest, readings for hydrogen sulphide were obtained within a quarter mile of the weir.

Bogle and Chandler had died within a quarter mile of the weir, right in the middle of the worst polluted area of the river!

I made contact with US-based Forensic Toxicologist Thomas Milby MD, and asked him to review the evidence I had compiled. Milby's expertise lay in determining harmful health effects associated with exposure to poisonous gases, including hydrogen sulphide. His interest in hydrogen sulphide poisonings dates back to the early 1960s in Cincinnati, Ohio. Employed as a medical officer in occupational health and safety, Milby was called to a frightening incident involving two of his colleagues, who had attempted to dispose of a cylinder of hydrogen sulphide:

> The valve was corroded and they couldn't open it safely, so they took it out to the countryside and shot a hole in it with a high-powered rifle to let it exhaust into the atmosphere. Since this gas was very highly compressed, it shot out at them, even though they were up-wind, like a fire hose. They saw it coming but before they could turn around and run, it was upon them. They fell down instantly. They were unconscious, began to convulse very heavily, and stopped breathing.[66]

Tom Milby MD

The men survived thanks to the actions of telephone linesmen, who had witnessed the incident from a nearby hill and provided very effective cardiopulmonary resuscitation (CPR). Tom Milby investigated the dramatic case. His findings were published in a respected medical journal. Since then, Tom has investigated more than one hundred cases of hydrogen sulphide poisoning, many of which were fatal. Having served on the National Academy of Science and the World Health Organisation Hydrogen Sulphide committees, his expertise was exactly what I needed.

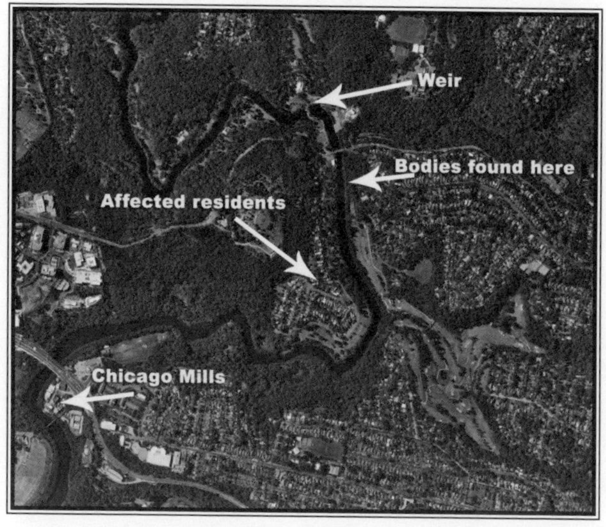

Despite his excellent credentials, I didn't tell Tom Milby the identity of the case or that there were two victims. I didn't want his opinion shaped by what he may have read on the internet. I merely told Tom that a person had been lying on an exposed riverbed at dawn beside a polluted river and that there were signs of disorientation and the victim had vomited and excreted. On reading the pollution history of the river, Dr Milby agreed that hydrogen sulphide poisoning was a distinct possibility. I felt I was heading in the right direction, but it was a question of, 'Where to from here?'

19. The Case Files

Dr Francis Camps, British forensic expert

Six weeks after I posted my letter to the police requesting access to their files on the Bogle-Chandler case, I received a telephone call from the Chief Inspector of the Unsolved Crimes Unit. This was one of those calls where I could tell from the tone of voice that I was wasting someone's valuable time.

'Unfortunately', he said, 'access is never given to the files of unsolved cases still considered open.' I expected as much. But with nothing to lose, I outlined what I had discovered in the previous weeks. I reminded him that the police and toxicologists who worked on the case believed that Bogle and Chandler had been poisoned. I explained that I had evidence that there was a source of a poisonous gas right next to where they died. We talked for an exhausting hour and a half, after which the Police Inspector said that he would recommend to the Deputy Commissioner of Police that an exception be made regarding access.

A few weeks later, I received a letter from the Deputy Commissioner inviting me to Police Headquarters where I was given unprecedented access to Bogle-Chandler case files, specifically, those related to the crime scene, pathology and scientific investigations.

My initial interest was in evidence that could either confirm or disprove my theory of hydrogen sulphide poisoning.

The police running sheet gave a detailed description of the police investigation on the day of the deaths. I learnt that police divers were called to search for evidence, such as phials or containers, which might have held a poison. I immediately contacted two of the divers named, who told me that they were unable to enter the water because of its dreadfully polluted condition.

A week and a half later, they returned, donned their wetsuits and air tanks and took to the river. Their search of the bottom relied on touch alone, they said. The water was still 'too murky to see anything'.

Access to the files also allowed me to track down Scientific Detective George Lindsay who had worked on the case for almost a month. Lindsay recalled the difficulties the divers had with the water conditions:

> This is one thing that we had to do, seeing the river was so close to where the bodies were. The divers couldn't see anything it was so muddy and polluted. It was a dirty river. They had to feel their way when they were diving and see if they could find anything in that vicinity that would help.

Some of the most intriguing case documents were responses from major law enforcement agencies and forensic laboratories around the world, including Interpol and Scotland Yard, to a request for help in solving the case.

One such reply came from Dr Francis Camps at the Department of Forensic Medicine, London Hospital Medical College. A leading pathologist in the 1950s and 1960s, Camps was the founder and president of the British Association of Forensic Medicine. Trained at Guy's Hospital Medical School, Camps later specialised in pathology, becoming a forensic medicine advisor to the Essex Police and an expert witness in many murder trials. Having carried out more than ten thousand post-mortems, he had seen just about every type of murder humans could perpetrate. His most celebrated case was the identification of six women found at the notorious 10 Rillington Place, which saw killer Reginald Christie go to the gallows.[67]

On reading the case notes about the Bogle-Chandler deaths, Dr Camps offered his considered opinion:

> From the position of the body of the man where he was found, it is clear that there must have been intervention by another person after consciousness and/or death. The

> presence of mud on the heels and backs of the shoes, suggests dragging. From the presence of cardboard cartons on the body of the woman, there is also intervention by another person. In both cases there is evidence of intervention by a person after death. It is also clear that it could not have been by either one or the other. Hence a third party must have done this. Whereas, it may be that this is the work of some disinterested party after death, the implication must be that it was done by someone who might well have been associated with the deaths. In this event it could have occurred either before (if unconscious) or after, if dead. If both were unconscious, then this would postulate some poison acting at the same time and therefore probably gaseous.

Bogle and Chandler had died from the effects of a gas; so postulated one of Britain's most revered pathologists. Camps offered three suggestions: carbon monoxide, which is produced by the exhaust of a car, and which would have been easily detectable as it changes the blood colour of victims to a cherry red. Similarly, hydrocyanic acid gas would have been easily picked up at autopsy due to its odour. That left carbon dioxide (CO_2), as his most favoured murder weapon. Indeed, carbon dioxide is considered the perfect murder weapon because it leaves no trace. Camps suggested that carbon dioxide could have been introduced into Bogle's car as 'dry ice' and the bodies taken to the location after they had died.

Unfortunately, the NSW Police had not supplied every detail about the case, leaving Dr Camps unable to appreciate the implausibility of the scenario. He was unaware that Bogle's car was parked in a very visible area about 150 metres from the location where the couple's bodies were found. Other cars were parked in the area. Their occupants would certainly have noticed people carrying or dragging dead bodies across the well-frequented road that passes over Fullers Bridge. Moreover, Bogle's car keys were found in the sun visor, exactly where he habitually left them, suggesting all was well as he and Mrs Chandler got out of their car.

From the case files, it was clear that CIB detectives took the opinion by Britain's top forensic expert seriously. Dry ice, carbon monoxide and other gases like fluorine and arsine were considered and tested for by the toxicologist. But a review of the master index revealed no consideration of hydrogen sulphide as a possible cause of death during the original investigation. The only mention of the gas was in a 1971 review of the case in which H_2S was discounted on a number of questionable counts, including that there was no obvious source of the gas.

A surprising aspect of the case files was the paucity of crime scene photographs. Of the dozen prints, there was no photograph of Mrs Chandler 'in situ'. I assumed that they had gone missing over the years.

Scientific Detective George Lindsay told me that he had taken over two dozen photos and as luck would have it knew where he could lay his hands on them. A few days later, he flew into Sydney carrying a suitcase of missing photographs, which he had stored in his garage! Amongst them, were images of Margaret Chandler lying on her back on the exposed riverbed directly below the riverbank. Beside her was the cardboard that had covered her body.

To my mind, the most important photographs show the exposed riverbed, directly below Bogle's body. In a line a metre out from the riverbank clearly visible were Mrs Chandler's shoes, her underpants and Dr Bogle's belt.

Victims' clothing

This had to be the location where the couple had lain down—a place where they would not be seen by passers-by; but as fate would have it, as close as one could be to the river and its poisonous store of hydrogen sulphide.

In 2006, Tom Milby flew to Australia to see the site for himself. A veteran of hundreds of cases, Tom assessed the scene and compared the police photos from 1963. He agreed that little had changed in four decades.

In his opinion, it was the worst place to be if hydrogen sulphide had been released from the river bottom. He described it as a bowl-shaped depression, lined with mangrove trees; a place where in the cool, still air of the morning the gas would be trapped. And cool it had been. Leicester Cotton, a guest at the Nash New Year's party, noted in the first chapter of his book, *The Bogle Mystery*: 'It was a cool night, with a faint mist in the air.'

Despite being the height of summer, Christmas Day had been the coldest since records began in the 1880's. The following days were also below normal temperature. Shadowed by easterly and westerly ridges, the river attracts far less sunlight than the surrounding neighbourhoods. On most nights a vapour hovers on the river surface, persisting up to an hour beyond dawn, sometimes up to half a metre in depth. A *Sun* newspaper reporter visited the river a few days after the Bogle-Chandler story broke: 'By night, and in the early morning, it is a dark way, enclosed by scratching lantana and dank with river mist.'

Until the sun rises and warms and circulates the air, it is not difficult to imagine hydrogen sulphide—a 'heavier than air' gas—enduring ominously in exactly the same way.

Amongst the Bogle-Chandler case files I came across the pathology reports, which the Coroner had blocked from public presentation at the Inquest. On reading them, I realised they had a direct impact on the hydrogen sulphide theory—and many other theories, for that matter.

While microbial examination revealed no evidence of 'complete sexual intercourse' having occurred, semen was found both on Dr Bogle's penis and the inside of his coat. Some form of sexual activity had taken place.

What the police made of this is not clear from the case files. But they had ample evidence from Mrs Fowler's testimony that Bogle was extremely careful not to make her pregnant, using both condoms and the 'withdrawal method'. On one occasion, when Mrs Fowler asked him to touch her, he replied, 'It's too dangerous, you don't know how fertile I am.'

Mrs Chandler's shoes

The pathology report implied that Dr Bogle and Mrs Chandler had not only had sex but were fit and well when they arrived at the river. It is impossible to envisage anyone who is suffering the ill effects of a poison partaking in sex.

Sexual activity also fits the location—a lovers' lane—and the state of the victims' clothing; both were half-naked and the Scientific Detectives found no evidence that either victim's clothing had been forcibly removed. By deduction, Bogle and Chandler were lying on the bed of the river and making love when they were struck down so rapidly and severely that they were unable to correct their clothing. Incredibly, there was no indication in the police report to the Coroner to suggest the investigators had reached this conclusion.

◆ ◆ ◆

I showed copies of all the pathology reports and autopsy findings to Thomas Milby:

> I read those two autopsy reports carefully and I saw nothing in either report that would, in my opinion, exclude the possibility of hydrogen sulphide as being the culprit that killed them. There was nothing I could see that would raise the probability that there was some other substance, some other chemical taken in and it was almost certainly, and I couldn't say this for sure but the probabilities are it was an inhaled gas, as opposed to a pill or something like that, because an inhaled gas tends to act very quickly, where a pill or something else does not.

But why wasn't hydrogen sulphide poisoning picked up at autopsy?

In a post-mortem examination, explained Dr Milby, it is difficult to determine hydrogen sulphide poisoning as a cause of death. Fatal, acute hydrogen sulphide intoxication produces no characteristic abnormalities other than pulmonary oedema (fluid in the lungs), congestion of the internal organs and scattered, small purplish spots on the skin or mucous membrane.

In some cases, Dr Milby explained, H_2S poisoning can leave a strange colouration in the blood and organs:

Sometimes an autopsy will show a greenish or purplish discolouration in the blood or organs. If an autopsy surgeon finds that the blood is purplish and finds no other cause for death, then that is extremely strong evidence for hydrogen sulphide being the lethal gas that caused the death. I don't know of any other substance, gas, liquid or whatever, that produces a greenish or purplish colour in the blood. It doesn't do it every time, but when it does, it is a fingerprint that identifies hydrogen sulphide.

The autopsy surgeons did not record a strange colouration of the blood. But, as I was to discover, somebody else did.

POISONS
ATOMIC & RADIUM LIQUID 344
SNAKE POISON. 346. 572.
HEAVY WATER 349.
DEATH RAY. 376.
ABRIN. 376.
PITJA BELING (POTSHERD) 388.
THALLIUM. 413.
CUT MELON. 413.
RADIOACTIVE ISOTOPE 431.
INJECTION OF AIR BUBBLES. 473.
GONYAULAX (PLANT POISON). 476.
PLASTIC BAG. 484.
CANTACIOUS DRUG. 509.
CHLORINE OR CHLORIDE. 560.
CYNOGAS (CYANIDE GAS) 560. 572.
TINSMITHS SOLDER ACID. 562.
OPIUM. 563.
DEADLY NIGHTSHADE (PLANT) 570.

List of tested poisons

20. Fingerprint

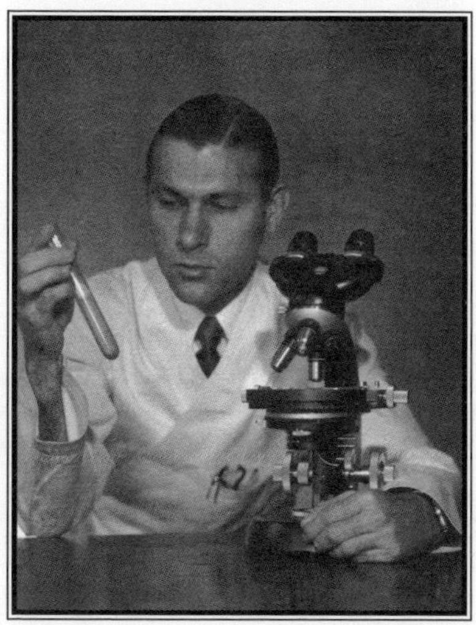

Viv Mahoney inspects blood sample

The slightly gravel-sounding voice at the end of the phone quipped, 'What took you so long?'

Access to the police case files enabled me to track down the Chief Toxicologist on the case, Vivian Mahoney. The directions he gave to his coastal Queensland home seemed overly detailed. I understood why as I tried to navigate his riverside street, which had more cul-de-sacs than probably any other road in Australia. His toxicology investigation into the deaths of Bogle and Chandler, I was to discover, was also marked by a series of dead-ends. And the fit, kindly looking man, who welcomed me at his door was still haunted by them.

In his search for the killer poison, Vivian Mahoney had spent more time on the case than anyone, but apparently I was the first person ever to enquire about his involvement.

Initially, he was reluctant to have his interview recorded on my small research camera, but finally agreed if it was only for note-taking purposes. There was another proviso; I was not to ask questions or interrupt. He wanted to tell his story as he remembered it. At this point, he had no knowledge of what I had found concerning the state of the river.

His account began on New Year's Day, 1963, recalling hearing about the mysterious deaths on the radio news. It ended thirteen months later; the night he ran out of tissue samples. Occasionally, a tear came to his eye. This had obviously been no routine case.

Mahoney transported me back to his toxicology lab, circa 1963. Every detail seemed authentically snap-frozen in time: meticulous explanations of the science involved; how tissues of the victims are prepared and analysed; and how the poisons are divided into two groups—organic and inorganic.

Mahoney said he found nothing in either victim's tissue samples, besides caffeine. Well almost. About fifty minutes into his intriguing monologue, he confessed something that he had not told anyone, apart from his superior, Mr Samuel Ogg:

> One thing I am certain of—and this might be stating the obvious—they both died from the same thing. I base this on the appearance of their blood. Both their bloods had a distinctive purple colouration.

It was a Eureka moment. I wanted desperately to interrupt to find out more about the blood, but Mahoney moved on to talk about testing for radioactivity. An hour later, when he had finished his story, I told Mahoney that, while I was no expert, I had a possible explanation for the discolouration. Over a cup of tea, I revealed my research into the Lane Cove River pollution and my evolving hydrogen sulphide theory. I said that I had heard of a similar blood discolouration in some victims.

From his body language, Mahoney seemed far from impressed. I felt I had crossed jurisdictional limits and backed off. What would I know about the rare art of toxicology? Indeed, I confessed that my knowledge of chemistry was limited to what I learnt while studying electronics in the 1970s. But I did have a world-renowned expert, who had told me about the blood discolouration issue.

At the airport, as I awaited my return flight to Sydney, I contacted Tom Milby by email and explained that we had a breakthrough—a purple discolouration had occurred in the haemoglobin of both victims. An email awaited me on my arrival home:

> Regarding the haemoglobin development, I am sure that you remember a paper I sent you titled: 'The purple

> brain death'. On page 200, Larson, et al. state: 'The most interesting gross autopsy finding consisted of a blue-green discolouration of the cut surface of the brain which was more accurately described by the autopsy surgeon as a light purple.' Another paper described autopsy findings in three young men fatally poisoned in an H_2S accident as: 'At autopsy, all had greenish cyanosis and greenish discolouration of the blood and viscera ... It is probable [say the authors] that some unstable sulphur-containing haemoglobin compound is responsible for the unusual haemic and visceral colours.' In my opinion, these authors are on the right track and the variable blood and tissue colours, reported in a helter-skelter fashion in the medical literature on hydrogen sulphide poisoning, is a function of this chemical instability.

Tom Milby was referring to a case in the United States in 1966, where three young men died after entering a sewer. At autopsy, all presented a greenish colour to the skin and greenish discolouration of both the blood and the soft organs of the body. The brain of one victim was strikingly greenish purple. No plausible explanation was offered for the presence of the strange colouration of organs or blood in any victim, other than a reaction between hydrogen sulphide and haemoglobin.

For a second opinion, Dr Milby put me in touch with another world authority on hydrogen sulphide poisoning, Dr Roger Smith, who had described the phenomenon in a scientific journal in the early 1960s.[68] Over the phone, Dr Smith agreed that the gas on occasion presents 'a green to purple coloration of blood'.

Over the coming months, I received seven long and thoughtful letters from Vivian Mahoney, in which he continually analysed and dissected the hydrogen sulphide theory. In his twelve years as a toxicologist, he had seen many deaths involving gases, but he had not come across one in which hydrogen sulphide was even suspected. While sceptical at first, Mahoney gradually came to appreciate that hydrogen sulphide may have been the cause of death. What seemed to sway him were the pathology reports in the police files concerning semen on Dr Bogle's coat and on his penis. He agreed that the couple could not have been suffering the ill effects of a poison when they arrived at the river. In fact, Mahoney was taken aback at learning this:

> It was not until this year—42 years later—that I am informed of the salient parts of the police report. And when I read those reports, I'm sort of a little annoyed that it wasn't available to me at that time, because it points me in a totally different direction. I'm annoyed that I spent a lot of time on poisons that didn't fit the circumstances time-wise or the state of the bodies!

With my cameraman in tow, I returned to Queensland to interview Viv Mahoney again. This time he went into more detail about the blood issue:

> When the two bloods came in with the rest of the organs, I immediately looked at them and I said to myself, 'Well,

> they've got a purple colouration those two bloods.' And I turned to my colleague, Sammy Ogg, and I said, 'Have a look at these bloods.' And he said, 'Well they seem a bit off colour, bit mauvey, bit purplish.' And I said, 'Yes, I was hoping you'd seen it before.' And I think his remark was, 'You know it's unusual for them to be off colour but with the bloods it depends sometimes how long they've been in the body and how they've been stored.' But I had only experienced some sort of darkening or lightening. It always worried me, the fact that they were both coloured purple. That to me indicated that they'd both died the same way.

Mahoney said that he set out to find the source of the strange discolouration:

> I went up to the Mitchell Library. It was only a couple of blocks from where I worked and I went through the literature on haemoglobins, hopefully trying to find something on the off-colouration and what caused it. I wasn't successful. I didn't find anything at that time that sort of explained an off-colour to the haemoglobin.

In 1963, Mahoney had no all-encompassing scanning technique to analyse blood, so he attempted to develop his own method to separate the purple compound. But after weeks of experimentation, he failed to isolate the mystery compound that caused the discolouration. While it was the only real clue discovered in the entire police and scientific investigation, he admitted that he did not mention it to the police. Four decades later, I supplied Bogle-Chandler case reports that he had not seen before along with scientific papers describing other deaths from H_2S. Mahoney then carried out his own research into the gas.

In a very encouraging letter, Viv Mahoney came to his own, somewhat colourful, conclusion about the events on New Year's morning, 1963:

> That leaves us with only one possibility. The instrument of death was right there in the depression where they lay down and acted very swiftly whilst they had sex and I am struggling to come up with anything other than gaseous. I can't imagine they drank at the stream or chewed anything before reclining. If I am right about the no foreplay, no hanging around and the substance acting in the middle of the act, those two people—admittedly in close contact—would have had to position their noses over a very heavy concentration of a very toxic gas. Tragically and amazingly, the poison struck suddenly at the point of assignation. If I knew that 42 years ago, and I was able to dig that up in the Mitchell Library, the case would have been over in a week. If I could have attributed that purple colour to something like H_2S ... I read plenty of records of it now, 42 years on, of people having cyanosis discolouration of that nature who have died from H_2S. It would seem to be a pointer, wouldn't it, on evidence that we have?

Evidence of Bogle's appetite for extra-marital liaisons in parks, Geoffrey Chandler's 'arrangement' with his wife, the seedy lovers' lane and the half-naked state of the bodies are vital to appreciating the events on New Year's morning. The victims were intent on making love. The pathology reports concerning fresh semen on his penis and a semen stain on the inside of his coat suggests that Bogle and Chandler were not suffering the effects of a poison when they arrived at the river. Chief Toxicologist Viv Mahoney concedes that the authorities failed the victims by not ensuring that he had all the facts of the case at his disposal:

> They should have got together and said, 'Look we're in trouble here. We're coming up negative all the time. Let's get together and let's compare notes.' I feel this Bogle and Chandler case could have been solved within weeks had there been cooperation between the three departments—the police, the pathologists that did the autopsy and myself, as the Government Analyst.

The suppression of the sexual aspects of the case to protect the victims' families from further anguish is one thing, but the failure to pass on pathology reports to the scientist charged with finding the cause of death meant that a fundamental piece of the puzzle was missing. There is no doubt in my mind that this was a major reason why the toxicology investigation stalled.

21. Master Of Deceit

In 1971, following a resurgence of media interest in the Bogle-Chandler mystery, the police asked the new Government Analyst, L. G. Clark, to review the case and examine some new theories that had been put forward by the public. As well as some bizarre poisons such as crocodile bile and coffin dust, gaseous vapour from river pollution was on the list.

In his report to the police, Clark discounted all the theories, including hydrogen sulphide, asserting that there was no recorded change in the colour of the blood. He also claimed there was no source of the gas, and even if there were, in an open environment it would not kill people. He noted:

> The suggestion is illogical, as the deceased would be required to be in a confined space. Other people would have suffered from these vapours from time to time but there has been no suggestion of this.[69]

Tom Milby described Clark's arguments as 'unsafe on all counts'. As a year-long scientific investigation proved, there was a massive reservoir of the gas within metres of the victims' mouths. Local records showed that the residents beside the river had experienced illnesses and breathing difficulties and millions of dead fish and eels had been gathered up and carted away in council trucks.

Clark's assumption that humans could not die from the gas in an open environment was also flawed. Hydrogen sulphide is one of the most common causes of asphyxiation in industrial accidents, and many fatalities have occurred in the open.

The highest recorded death toll occurred in Poza Rica, Mexico in 1950, when an oil refinery pipeline was accidentally vented, releasing hydrogen sulphide gas into the air. In normal circumstances, the gas might have dissipated, but a temperature inversion kept it low to the ground. Twenty-two people died and 320 people were hospitalised. Exposure levels were estimated to have reached up to 2,000 parts per million, two and a half times the concentration required to kill a human being.

In Japan in 1994, four adult men were found dead in an artificial lake, which was being used to raise fish. Autopsies revealed the men had drowned, but investigators discovered 'the concentration of hydrogen sulphide gas at the scene was estimated as having been nearly fatal'.[70]

In 1995, in Savannah, Georgia, explosions rocked a commercial bulk liquid chemical storage and transfer facility. The damage was catastrophic, with fire fighters taking almost three days to put out the fire. Soon after, 2,000 residents within one-half mile of the facility were forced to evacuate, when chemicals began leaking from storage tanks and reacted to produce toxic hydrogen sulphide gas. Three hundred people were hospitalised suffering from hydrogen sulphide exposure.

A case with marked similarities to the Bogle-Chandler case occurred at Yellowstone National Park in the United States in 2004, not with humans, but animals. While on patrol, park rangers stumbled on five bison lying dead beside a river. There was no doubt the bison died as a group and very rapidly. According to the park's geologist, the animals were grazing and resting in a snow-free ground depression along the Gibbon River, near multiple geothermal gas vents. Cool, still air from a cold front passing through the area probably caused the geyser basin's steam and toxic gases to remain close to the ground, overwhelming the animals. A combination of hydrogen sulphide and carbon dioxide was thought to be the cause of death. Both gases, the geologist said, 'accumulate in topographically low areas on cold, calm nights because they are denser than air'. Although rare, incidents such as this were not unheard of in the park's history.[71]

As these cases prove, hydrogen sulphide deaths do occur in the open if the air is cool and still.

In his 1971 review of the Bogle-Chandler case, Clark also stated that the post mortem examination showed no other signs that 'excess hydrogen sulphide could be the cause of death'. Clark was obviously unaware that hydrogen sulphide poisoning is difficult to pinpoint in a post mortem examination.

Clark added that there was no 'darkening of the blood'. Darkening of the blood is not a typical finding in H_2S deaths, though a green to purplish colouration can occur.

According to Vivian Mahoney, Dr Clark had not worked on the original Bogle-Chandler investigation and after finding scant paperwork on the case, telephoned him for advice. Mahoney said Clark did not mention hydrogen sulphide nor question him about the blood of the victims.

◆ ◆ ◆

If hydrogen sulphide was the instrument of death, why, I am continually asked, was the couple not put off the location by the smell of hydrogen sulphide? Bogle was a scientist; surely he would have recognised the gas's highly distinctive odour and realised the danger?

Tom Milby, who has acted as an expert witness in many legal cases involving hydrogen sulphide poisoning, suggests the killer gas is a master of deceit:

> Hydrogen sulphide is generally known as rotten egg gas because it is generated when an egg goes bad. It has several characteristics that make it anywhere from annoying to deadly toxic. Most of us can pick up the smell of hydrogen sulphide at extremely low concentrations of way less than one part per million. It's annoying because it doesn't smell very good but it doesn't take any serious toxicity on until it reaches about fifty to a hundred parts per million. Once it gets up to about a hundred and fifty parts per million, which is not very high, it anaesthetises the nerves we have in our nose that are responsible for picking up odours. So you don't smell it.

In high concentrations, a victim can be oblivious to the fact that the gas is even present:

> If it gets into the two or three hundred parts per million, then it begins to take an effect on the brain. Hydrogen sulphide works by causing chemical asphyxiation, defined simply as an inability to get oxygen to the brain. When you inhale hydrogen sulphide gas, it goes immediately into the blood through the lung, without hurting the lung, without even knowing you're breathing it. And if it gets in a high enough concentration in the blood, it will begin to close off oxygen to the brain. The brain is the organ in our body that requires more oxygen than any other organ. And it's like putting a plastic bag over the brain. Sometimes the concentration in the air is so high that a person who comes into contact will fall immediately to the ground.

Of the victims who do survive, very few recall smelling any odour. Rescuers, too, can also succumb because they have no hint that the gas is present. In the United States in 1946, a Coroner arrived at a farm to inspect the death of a boy near a cesspool, but did not realise that he too was in danger until he walked away from the scene. The boy's father had also collapsed but later recovered.

The Coroner reported:

> In the accident there was apparently no awareness of any unusual odours. On being questioned after recovery, the father stated that he did not notice the odour, when

> it was described to him. Furthermore, when I visited the scene shortly after the boy was pronounced dead, I did not note the odour. It was only after I had walked approximately 50ft from the cesspool that the nature of the gas became apparent.[72]

At Rotorua in New Zealand, hydrogen sulphide gas is continuously released into the atmosphere from its famous mud pools and hot springs. Since European settlement, scores of people have died after inhaling the gas. This tragic wealth of fatalities has enabled researchers to appreciate both the astonishing killing capacity of H_2S and what some victims experience. In April 1962, Mr R. A. Bird was standing with his six-year-old-son, Warren, watching a bore filling a pool at the Old Boys' Rugby Club rooms in Te Ngae Road:

> The bore had been going about a minute when suddenly Warren dropped. I threw him outside on the ground and applied artificial respiration. But it was no use and I thought he had gone. His stomach was as hard as concrete. Then I thought of mouth-to-mouth resuscitation. It was a tough job opening Warren's jaws, which had gone tight. But I got his mouth open and forced breath down his mouth. After a while he came to, screaming.[73]

Rotorua survives on tourism, so it comes as no surprise that the local authorities have been prone to downplaying the risks. They certainly do not mention that the odd odour people notice on arrival is that of a serial killer, which can strike at random. In the majority of fatalities, very little documentary proof can be obtained. But in some cases, the cause of death cannot be disputed.

In Rotorua in 1962, hydrogen sulphide scored a double killing. In their one-roomed flat Harold McCutcheon, 54, a retired railway worker, and Violet Clement, 45, were found dead by the proprietor of the flats. Lethal concentrations of hydrogen sulphide gas were found at floor and bed levels in the flat. Its source was not immediately apparent, but was finally traced to a leaky heating radiator. At that time, geothermal heating units pumped hot, gas-laden water from below ground directly into heating radiators in Rotorua living rooms and bedrooms. A leaking radiator in a badly ventilated room was a lethal weapon. Laws were subsequently passed to ensure that only fresh, town-supply water heated in a geothermal heat exchanger was circulated through domestic heating pipes and radiators.

The most high profile case in Rotorua was that of a veteran Austrian actress. In 2000, Eleanor Umlauf-Ruprecht was talking on the phone in her Sulphur City Hotel room when she collapsed. The hotel manager was alerted, rushed to the room and found her dead. The Sulphur City Hotel is located 300 metres from any known source of the gas. The Rotorua Coroner, David Dowthwaite, said he was unable to resolve how the woman came to be exposed to the high level of hydrogen sulphide gas at such a distance, but said that there was little doubt she had died from hydrogen sulphide poisoning.

In 2009, the Coroner of Rotorua, Dr Wallace Bain, investigated two suspected H_2S poisoning deaths. One case involved Phillip Binns, who died in Pinelands Motor Lodge hot pool in 2007. The other was that of 88-year-old, Mr Philip Ham, who was found dead in a hot pool at the Fernleaf Motel in 2008.

Ham's daughter had accompanied him to the pool as she had done on many previous occasions. In his official report, Coroner Bain recorded her terrifying experience:

> She said she got in the pool, and her father always sat in one position, and she sat opposite. They had the water up to their necks. She said within seconds he started exercising his legs in the water. She did that also and then all of a sudden she felt peculiar in the neck and the face. She said it was a new sensation and it was so unusual that she immediately stood up. She said the sensation was different to feeling hot. She had extra beats in her heart, and she could feel her neck and her face were not right. She wondered in fact whether she was having a heart attack and she simply wanted out. She stood up, with her back to her father, and bent over the little concrete wall. She went back to the steps. She said to her father she was getting out, but he did not answer. She had never left him before. She went back to the motel and got changed, and she was surprised her father had not come back and she then went back to the pool where she found him (dead).[74]

The Inquest heard that tests were carried out at the location of Mr Ham's death, and 'while the levels of hydrogen sulphide were elevated, they were not highly elevated to the extent of presenting an immediate hazard'.

But expert witnesses, including the toxicologist, all concluded that H_2S was the cause of death in both the Ham and Binns cases. In his findings, delivered in March 2010, the Coroner made some interesting observations about the unpredictability of the deadly gas:

> What is clear from this Inquest is that hydrogen sulphide poisoning can be fatal and its onset is very quick. It has occurred over the years and whilst thousands of bathers have had no problem, there is still that wildcard risk factor ... Hydrogen sulphide poisoning...can and does occur and strikes at random.

The common thread connecting virtually every case of hydrogen sulphide poisoning is the lack of a warning of exposure. At high concentrations, the victim does not notice any odour before becoming unconscious. In that sense, hydrogen sulphide is indeed a master of deceit.

22. Death by the River

On an unseasonably cool New Year's morning in 1963, there appears to have occurred a rare but highly dangerous convergence of circumstances never contemplated by the police.

At around 4.05 am Bogle drove off from the Nash party. A party guest told detectives that he seemed to be alone in his car. But between 4.20 and 4.30 am Bogle's vehicle pulled up at a well-known tail-light alley alongside the Lane Cove River and there was a woman in the seat next to him—Mrs Margaret Chandler. There can be little doubt that they had romance in mind. Margaret had an 'arrangement' with her husband Geoffrey, that she could take Bogle as her lover 'should the opportunity arise'. This was such an opportunity.

But the appearance of a scruffy looking, one-armed voyeur, Kenneth Challis, appears to have prompted Dr Bogle to move his vehicle closer to Fullers Bridge and look for somewhere more private.

Bogle went to the boot of his car and removed a carpet square. The couple then crossed Millwood Avenue and walked south down the bush track that ran beside the river. It is difficult to imagine a woman wearing her best dress in such a rubbish-strewn location; but as other women had testified to police, outdoor lovemaking was Dr Bogle's modus operandi.

It was twilight, with the sun due to find the river at around 4.50 am, some 15 minutes away. They looked for somewhere they would not be seen and clambered down the bank to the riverbed. As fate would have it, the tide that morning was low. The riverbed was relatively dry and covered with a soft carpet of she-oak needles. Further out, a thicket of semi-submerged mangroves created a snug, private cocoon.

Bogle dropped his car mat onto the riverbed, removed his jacket and positioned it over the carpet for extra comfort.

Toxicologist, Vivian Mahoney:

> They were mature people there for but one purpose and to me that would have pointed to little foreplay. They were in a dirty hollow on the bed of a not too clean river. A matter of 'enough with the frivolity', their approach would have been let us get at it and leave. It was now becoming lighter. Why would you hang around? That is why I say the substance acted very quickly as they were doing the act.

Indeed, while making love and breathing heavily, something overcame them suddenly and they found themselves suffocating. Margaret Chandler in some way made it to her feet and attempted to locate her underwear, but in her delirium, and possibly partial-blindness, she picked up Bogle's underpants by mistake. Gasping vainly for air, Dr Bogle excreted as he tried to edge himself backwards up onto the bank.

Tom Milby:

> They would have become disorientated and acted in ways that were not helpful to them. That is to say they might have tried to get out, but stumbled backwards—all sorts of things that you can conceive of someone who is semi-unconscious.

Desperate for air, Margaret staggered across the riverbed, grazing her bare arms and legs on mangrove branches. She fell to her knees, excreted, and stumbled a little further, scratching her nose on foliage before collapsing in a hollow beside the riverbank.

On the riverbank, Bogle crawled a little, convulsed and vomited before collapsing.

Neither victim was able to correct their clothing—testimony to the speed, synchronicity and acuteness of the event. Both lay comatose, but with their brains starved of oxygen, both finally succumbed.

Tom Milby:

> Lethality takes a few minutes to occur, it doesn't occur instantly. If there had been a thousand parts per million in that 'bowl', they would have not gotten out of there but there wasn't. There was something less than that, but not much less. My estimation would be around 700 parts per million of hydrogen sulphide.

The police arrived at the scene between five and five and a half hours later. While the police divers noted that the river was too polluted to enter, there is no mention in police records of any odour. However, newspaper reporter Bill Jenkings, who turned up just before midday, wrote that the stifling summer heat 'magnified the putrid odour of excrement and death'. After only six or seven hours, a body would not have decomposed sufficiently to reek of 'death'. What the reporter may have noticed was residual, low-level hydrogen sulphide coming from the river. But is there anyway to prove it?

In 2006, following the broadcast of my documentary *Who Killed Dr Bogle & Mrs Chandler?* two people came forward who claimed they were at the river on New Year's day. Their astonishing testimonies suggest that an environmental incident had occurred that day.

After leaving a New Year's party in Auburn, 19-year-old Lindsay Mitchell and two friends had decided to drive to Manly Beach for a swim. Exhausted from the celebrations, they stopped at the dusty car park near Fullers Bridge to sleep the rest of the night in the car. Around dawn, Mitchell woke with a thirst and got out of the car to look for water:

> I saw the river and I thought well I don't know whether it is salt water or fresh water, but I'll go down and have a look and see if I can get a drink. As I approached the riverbank, I noticed that the river was heavily polluted. It wasn't flowing. It was stagnant. It was putrid. It had lots of debris floating on the top, like sticks and leaves

> and there were dead fish floating belly-up on the surface of the water. And as I got closer I noticed there was this incredible smell. The water stank. I felt like I couldn't breath. And I thought there is no way I am drinking that water, I'll die of thirst first, so I turned around and went back to the car.

Several weeks later, Mitchell responded to a call by police for owners of cars parked in the area on New Year's morning to come forward. He called Chatswood detectives and gave the car owner's details, but didn't mention his experience that morning.

North Ryde resident, Derek Foster, was at the Lane Cove River that afternoon:

> My brother-in-law, Mick, came to visit us at our home with his family in a brand-new company car, which he brought over to show us. We had lunch then later in the afternoon we decided to go to Chatswood to get Chinese takeaway for dinner. Mick said he would give us a run in his new car. The children wanted to take Fritz, our crossbred dog, so off we went to Chatswood via Delhi Road. We had heard the news about the bodies found by the river. When we got to Fullers Bridge it was quiet. We parked in the parking area in Lady Game Drive and walked onto the bridge to have a look down the river to see if we could see anything. There was a policeman guarding the entrance to the track, which led to the golf course. There was no activity that we could see, so after a few minutes we decided to resume our journey. I whistled the dog and he came running from the direction

> of the river bank where the policeman was, and, as we all got back into the car, we all became aware of a smell like rotten eggs and realised that the dog had been rolling in something bad. We went to Chatswood, got the Chinese food and couldn't get home quickly enough. We could hardly stand the smell. Mick was furious and cleaned the back of his car as best as he could. I hosed the dog down, but the smell was hard to get rid of. It was a family joke for a long time, that's probably how I remember what happened so clearly.

I telephoned Mr Foster's ex-wife to verify the story. She had not spoken to Mr Foster since their divorce. She relayed to me exactly the same story, adding that she had never smelled 'anything so vile in her life'.

Both men provided me with statutory declarations. Their stories suggest that a hydrogen sulphide event occurred at the Lane Cove River on New Year's morning, 1963. It appears that Dr Bogle and Mrs Chandler were in the worst of locations at a critical time of day and as they made love, breathing heavily, they became victims of the toxic gas's killing ways.

23. Dark Secret

The outstanding question is how the bodies of Bogle and Chandler came to be covered in such an unusual manner. Four decades on, that question can also be answered.

Two and a half weeks after the deaths, CIB detectives told the press that there was no doubt that a 'third person' was involved. Their only suspects were the one-armed former carpenter, Raymond Challis, and the 58-year-old master butcher/greyhound trainer, Eddy Batiste.

While Challis contacted the police voluntarily, Batiste only came forward after a description of his green and white Ford Customline vehicle appeared in the media. That led the police to believe Mr Batiste might have had something to hide.

In his interview with detectives, Batiste said that he had left his home at Hunters Hill around 4.15 am. As he crossed Fullers Bridge, he heard the time announced on his car radio, 'It is now 27 minutes to five.' To the left of the bridge, he noticed Dr Bogle's Ford Prefect in the car park but didn't see anyone in the car. Batiste said he then drove down an upper trail to the golf course—not the lower, riverside track, which Bogle and Chandler had taken.

On arrival at the golf course, he said he 'slipped' his champion greyhound dogs then returned to his car. Batiste swore he did not see the couple dead or alive. At the Coronial Inquest, he gave matching testimony. That seemed to be the end of his worth to the investigation.

Eddy Batiste with champion greyhound

Eddy Batiste died in 1976. In 2006, I tracked down three of his children. One of his sons recalled Eddy arriving home on New Year's Morning, 1963, at about 6 am—two hours before teenager Michael McCormick first came across the body of Dr Bogle. He said Eddy was 'in a very agitated state'.

The following day, 2 January, Eddy commented on the breaking story in the newspapers and said that he had been near the location the previous morning. His son maintained a suspicion that Eddy did find the half-naked couple and covered them. I asked why he held that suspicion. He described his father as a 'moralist' who had an aversion to the sight of bare human flesh. A very strange obsession for a butcher, indeed, but it was a possible explanation as to why the bodies were covered in such a bizarre manner.

I visited Eddy Batiste's daughter, Mary, and her husband, Ron. They offered another perspective.

> Ron: I think the first time we heard about it was from Mary's father and he said, 'Have a look in the paper and you'll see about a great murder or suicide or something.' He said that, 'I happened to exercise me dogs right past where it happened.'
>
> Mary: His car had been identified there so he rang the police and said, 'Yes that was me and I exercised the dogs there.'
>
> Myself: Did he see anything down there that morning?
>
> Mary: Well, he never mentioned it to me. Being on the top track he couldn't have seen them, because they were beside the lower track.
>
> Myself: Your brother told me that your father came home in an agitated state that morning.
>
> Mary: Yes, my brother thought he came home a little bit distressed. I thought it may have been because of all the cars there; it was New Year and there could have been

parties and it was a lovers' lane, as they say. That might have upset him, because he used to like to be on his own and just slip the dogs quickly and get away quickly.

Myself: If your father had seen the bodies, wouldn't he have admitted it to the police?

Mary: I don't think he would have told the police. He was a very secretive man.

Mary then went digging for something in another room, returning with a 1977 edition of the *National Greyhound News* magazine, which contained her father's obituary. A few paragraphs in, it stated boldly that Eddy Batiste was the person who 'found the bodies' of Dr Bogle and Mrs Chandler! Was this merely poetic license or had Eddy confessed to someone in the greyhound world?

My attempts to find anyone within the greyhound industry who had been closely acquainted with Eddy Batiste proved unsuccessful.

But a week before the broadcast of my documentary I received a tantalising phone call. At the end of the line was a woman with 'new information' about the case. Now in her mid-50s, Lorraine Blackwood had seen a promotion for the film on television and decided it was time for her and her mother, Joan, to get a family secret 'off their chests'. As the film had not yet been broadcast, they had no idea what the documentary contained.

In 1963, 11-year-old Lorraine lived in Gladesville, the same suburb I grew up in, which lies about five kilometres from where the bodies were found. A few days after the Bogle-Chandler story broke in 1963, Lorraine, along with her younger sister and a local boy, set off from home to explore a small area of bushland at the lower end of Westminster Road, Gladesville. On a rocky outcrop beside a storm water outlet, they found a woman's bone-coloured handbag.

Lorraine Blackwood's mother, Joan, recalled the children returning home and noticing the bag on the boy's arm:

> I said, 'Where did you get that handbag?' and he said, 'Lorraine and I found it down by the big tree over the stormwater channel.' And I said, 'You'd better give it to me to have a look.'

Inside the bag, she found a handkerchief, cosmetics and two bottles of white pills prescribed to a Mrs

Margaret Chandler from a Croydon Park pharmacy. Mrs Blackwood panicked:

> And I thought 'Oh, my God!' My four children were all young and I was frightened with my husband in America at the time. So I put it in the garbage, and it went to the tip.

Lorraine Blackwood confirmed that her mother seemed terrified about the public notoriety their involvement in the case could bring:

> You have to remember this was the 1960s. It was a different place and different time. This was a horrific crime with a lot of strange stories and rumours circulating. Because my mother had four young children to fend for and her sailor husband was overseas, Mum decided she didn't want her family caught up in a murder case that was front-page news.

At the time, detectives were puzzled as to why Mrs Chandler didn't have a handbag with her at the river. For a woman of that era to attend a party without one was highly unusual. Scientific detectives considered the mystery solved when they found a brown handbag containing Mrs Chandler's licence, money, cosmetics and a house-key in a suitcase at the Chandler home.

But the suitcase, which also contained clothing for the children, had been at Margaret's parents' home in Granville that night.

Detectives ascertained that Margaret had arrived at the Nash party with two pairs of shoes. A brown pair was found on the riverbed. A bone pair was found in the Chandler car—so it made sense that she had left her Croydon home with two handbags to match her two pairs of shoes.

The question was how did Margaret's bone handbag end up five kilometres from the crime scene? I made inquiries with an elderly couple living adjacent to the location where the children found the bag. They said that an ex-boxer, who worked at the local council tip, resided in the house opposite the stormwater channel. His name had a very familiar ring to it—Bill Batiste—the same surname as that of the greyhound trainer! If this was a coincidence, it was an extraordinary one.

Bill Batiste was Eddy Batiste's nephew. He lived only a few blocks away from the greyhound trainer's home in Hunters Hill. Indeed, Eddy would have passed by there on his journey home from the Lane Cove River.

But this astonishing story raises more questions than it answers.

Why did Eddy take the bag in the first place, then dispose of it? Did it contain money? Didn't he suspect that it belonged to the woman on the riverbed? On his way home, a journey of little more than ten minutes, did he finally make the connection and panic? Perhaps he suddenly grasped that someone might have seen his car at the river. Or did he realise that by removing evidence from a 'crime scene', he would be considered a suspect in the case?

Forty years on, it seemed to me to have been an extremely risky place to dispose of the bag. If Mrs Blackwood had gone to the police rather than placing the handbag in the rubbish bin, the investigators may have put 'two and two' together, connecting the bag to his nephew and then Eddy, himself. The greyhound trainer certainly would have had a great deal of explaining to do.

I contacted Eddy's daughter Mary who was taken aback by these revelations. At the same time she was adamant that it could not have been attributed to her cousin, Bill Batiste. 'He kept to himself,' she said, and would not have accompanied her father to the river to train his dogs. While it was unlikely that a man walking his racing dogs was the killer, the police would undoubtedly have used the handbag discovery to force Eddy Batiste to confess. If he admitted that he had seen the bodies and had covered them, he may have faced a prison term.

Frustratingly, so much valuable information about the victims was lost by Batiste's actions, such as whether they were alive or dead when he stumbled upon them.

In 2008, through family connections, I was introduced to a 91-year-old pathologist who had worked in the greyhound racing industry since the Second World War. In the 1960s he was a Chief Stipendiary Steward charged with keeping the notoriously corruptible sport as clean as possible. He had not seen my documentary and had no knowledge of any aspect of it. I asked him if he'd ever come across Eddy Batiste. He said he had known Eddy very well and described him as a 'gentleman and a brilliant trainer'. In fact, they used to travel together to country race meetings. Without prompting, he quipped that Eddy had something to do with the Bogle-Chandler Case.

Indeed, a few weeks after the story broke in 1963, Eddy had telephoned him:

> Eddy said, 'You know those two bodies down on the Lane Cove River? I found them. Both dead.' I said, 'How did you know?' He said, 'It was obvious, mate. I was walking the dogs when one of them must have heard a rustle in the bushes.' Eddy said his dog pulled him toward the river where he found the naked body of a woman. He said he was embarrassed about it. He mentioned something about beer cartons there, but he didn't say he covered her. He said, 'The bodies weren't together. You've no idea—there were faeces everywhere in the trees.'

While Batiste did not tell the police this story, he had told his associates in the greyhound world. The Steward added: 'Everyone thought it was a joke, you know, Eddy finding a couple of corpses!'

Eddy Batiste had lied to the police. He had seen the bodies. The discovery of Mrs Chandler's handbag, abandoned in the vicinity of his nephew's home, suggests that Eddy Batiste was the person who disposed of it there on his way home from the river.

The Steward said Batiste was a good enough fellow, but 'didn't do everything by the book'. In his opinion, he was the type of man who would have taken the handbag for the money. He also recalled Eddy Batiste sounding nervous on the phone and saying, 'The coppers said I did it!'

So why didn't Batiste go straight to the police?

Often witnesses to an accident or a crime fear becoming involved, but I could not help wondering if there was a far more serious reason for not cooperating with the police; something in his background, perhaps. That set me on a new phase of research.

I discovered that the Batiste name had been dragged through the Courts on at least three occasions. One of his brothers had died accidentally in a drunken fight at the hands of his cousins. Another brother, who was chronically addicted to methylated spirits, stole holy items from the local Catholic Church. Was it Eddy's unsavoury family history that made him fearful of dealing with the law?

While searching other stories of human drama on the Lane Cove River, I discovered a far more compelling explanation. In a Sydney newspaper, I came across a simple, poignant memorial notice that spoke of a family's heartbreak:

> All is dark within our home;
> Lonely are our hearts today,
> For the one we loved so dearly,
> Has forever passed away

On the 2 January 1906, 57 years almost to the day before the deaths of Dr Bogle and Mrs Chandler, two sisters from the Sydney suburb of Riverview, Irene Hyde, 14, and Catherine Hyde, 12, took a ferry across the Lane Cove River to visit relatives at Hunter's Hill. Only one would return.

In the course of that holiday afternoon, tragedy would befall the Hyde family. After playing with their young cousins for two hours, the girls said their farewells and headed home for dinner.

Gallantly, two of their male cousins chaperoned the sisters down to the Lane Cove River to catch the ferry. Eager and able, the boys offered to row them across the river in a small punt. But at mid-stream a larger boat steamed by at full speed. Seconds later its wake swamped the punt, tossing the four young people into the violent, foaming wash. Although a good swimmer, Irene struggled and grabbed onto one of the boys.

Onshore, a youth by the name of Ritchie witnessed the accident. He quickly manned a boat and rowed with all his might to the scene. By the time he arrived, one of the boys was disappearing under the water. By his brave actions, Ritchie saved the lad then gathered the older brother and the younger girl, Catherine, onto his boat. But Irene could not be found.

Working with hurricane lamps, the police searched the Lane Cove River into the night, but failed to find the missing girl. The following morning, the police continued the search and finally recovered Irene's body from the river. The next day, the Coroner interviewed the children and the rescuer before recording, 'death by drowning'.

According to newspaper reports, the surname of the relatives the Hyde girls had visited was 'Batiste'.[75] I contacted Mary Batiste to see if there was a connection. She confirmed that the 10-year-old boy whom Irene had clutched onto for dear life and almost drowned was her father, the future greyhound trainer, Eddy Batiste.

It was yet another fascinating revelation. Over half a century earlier, Eddy Batiste had been a central player in another tragedy on the Lane Cove River!

Eddy and his brother had assisted with the search and had witnessed the police covering Irene Hyde's lifeless body with a blanket. Could this distressing event in Eddy's early life—involving a police investigation and a Coronial Inquest—explain why Eddy covered the bodies?

One can only imagine what detectives would have thought had they discovered Batiste had been involved in another death on the Lane Cove River. But as fortune or fate would have it, police records of the event had been destroyed by 1963, and Eddy's dark secret went with him to his grave.

24. Damage

'When I die, it will be a shipwreck and as when a huge ship sinks, many people all around will be sucked down with it', so contemplated the famous egocentric artist Pablo Picasso.

Similarly, those closely associated with the Bogle-Chandler case were dragged down by the tragedy. A wife, a husband, six young children, mothers, fathers, brothers, friends, colleagues, acquaintances and lovers have suffered in the wake of the events of New Year's Day, 1963.

In March 1963, Vivienne Bogle buried her husband in a small suburban cemetery at North Ryde, less than a mile away from where he had died. None of the Bogle children were present. Following the Coronial Inquest, Mrs Bogle flew out of Sydney for New Zealand. Her two eldest children had been sent ahead to avoid, one expects, the continuing onslaught of publicity. Sedately dressed in a winter suit and hat, ground staff assisted her and her two youngest children onto the plane. Waving to her well-wishers, she put on a brave face. On board, with her 10-month-old baby in her arms, she reportedly wept.

Margaret Chandler was cremated and her ashes

interred at the Northern Suburbs Crematorium, directly overlooking the Lane Cove River.

One can only imagine the distress Margaret's death caused her parents and brothers. My contact with her brothers has been limited to a difficult telephone call in 2006 to warn them that my film was going to be broadcast.

Newspapermen continued their pursuit of Geoffrey Chandler. In 1964, they tracked him down to his parents' holiday house on the Queensland coast. A fistfight ensued and a camera was broken.

Geoffrey Chandler:

> It's enough to lose a mother; you can cope with that. But then when you have it all blown up into a national mystery, and then you have it salaciously represented year after year after year after year, it's a wonder they didn't all go off their trolleys. You see, the bloody newspapers, the *Daily Mirror* in particular, every year would have a full page or a double page spread of pictures and rehash of what happened on New Year 1963. And the whole of their school had this refreshed every year! Did these newspaper people think of that sort of thing? No, no, no. The fact that they have survived all that, albeit with emotional damage: I'm surprised that the damage is not greater. Plus the fact that I was so much on the defensive by all of this and that I probably failed. If I'd been more honest and not running so scared of the whole situation, things would have been better. But then that's 'what if?' For us all, life is not as it was. Life is not as it could have been.

The police had no evidence with which to charge Geoffrey Chandler, but the weight of public opinion was against him. Any hope he may have had of returning to a normal life was illusory. He had attempted to keep connections with Margaret's family. While his two boys—Gareth and Sean—were welcome, Geoffrey was not. He accepted that the Morphetts blamed him for their daughter's death. Margaret's parents suggested it would be better for the two boys if other family members adopted them. Geoffrey held his ground, but ultimately found it difficult to raise his two children and they suffered the consequences:

> As for the boys, the emotional damage has been quite intense, quite deep. Gareth, the elder boy, suffered acute feelings of deprivation. Half his recognisable world had disappeared, and he was terribly afraid of losing the other half, his father. Despite being surrounded by a loving group of relatives, he hated to let me out of his sight. Sometimes young women came to look after all three of us out of kindness or for accommodation, in return for which they would cook and clean. Several came out of affection for me; some saw the situation as a cause worth dedicating themselves to, at least temporarily. One of these women, who cared for the children as if they had been her own, simply took pity on me one night when, exhausted by my own difficulties, I broke down and wept in front of her. She moved into the house and generously helped me at a time when everything else was total disaster. But she left, too, and someone else had to be found. This succession of strangers was bad for the children. It got us nowhere.

At first, Chandler's employer, the CSIRO, was supportive, but as time went on he realised that his career trajectory had been curtailed. In 1967, after fifteen years of working in radio physics, Chandler resigned and took over a publishing company, which produced neighbourhood newspapers. He had avoided, even despised the press for years, now he had joined their club. Moreover, he capitalised on his notoriety in *So You Think I Did It?*, a slim paperback ghost-written by award-winning journalist and poet Elizabeth Riddell, and published by Rupert Murdoch.

In 2005, I took Geoffrey Chandler to the place where his wife had died. He had only once been there since 1963, and did not know the exact location or the details of what really occurred down there. I told him the sorry history of the river and how I believed hydrogen sulphide had killed his wife and Dr Bogle. The man with the scientific mind knew of the gas and its lethal ways. He shook his head as he looked out to the benign-looking waterway. A few months later, I interviewed Chandler for my documentary:

> The police in Sydney in those days were relatively innocent in their inexperience in the state of forensic art. Things have advanced since then. People weren't aware 40 years ago to the extent that they are today of the effects of environmental pollution. It's taken you 40 years to come up with this hydrogen sulphide theory, which in the light of your investigations and other people's investigations of similar sorts of documented cases in other parts of the world, seems to stand up to close examination. It seems

> highly likely that they died through hydrogen sulphide poisoning. It seems completely feasible; the most realistic and sensible theory on the cause of death that has come up in the last 20 or 30 years. It makes it just an accident. It's something terribly, terribly unfortunate. It takes it away from the paranormal to the normal.

Following a nine-month illness, Geoffrey Chandler died in August 2009. I spoke to him a few days before his passing. There was no deathbed confession. He was a man with a sound alibi who, in the eyes of the police and public, acted strangely blameworthy. He had lived a life of extremes and contradictions. Opposed to convention and conservatism, he suffered the consequences of being different. No one could doubt his intelligence. Yet his brilliance compounded people's belief that he could kill two people without leaving a trace. He was a strong, striking, tall, virile man who loved women, yet he treated them uncaringly, especially the mother of his children. At his funeral wake, two of a long string of women whom he later became involved with candidly pondered what they had seen in him.

Geoffrey Chandler was typical of a fair percentage of Australian men of his era. Today, such a lack of emotion and irregular social behaviour would possibly come under scrutiny at an early age. But way back then no-one really focused on Geoffrey Chandler's personal traits until the day he opened his door to the police and a life of notoriety. At Chandler's funeral, his oldest son, Gareth, told it as it was. When his mother died, he said, he and his brother lost both their parents.

The police investigation took its toll on many of those who became embroiled in the case. The sultry blonde Pamela Logan, Chandler's lover, was painted as the femme fatale in the story. A nightclub entertainer paid enthusiastic homage to her in song with 'I'm In Love With Miss Logan'. Soon after the inquest, with her reputation in tatters, she allegedly departed Australia for America.

The reputation of Dr Bogle's lover, Mrs Margaret Fowler, had also taken a battering. The fact that her evidence was suppressed at the inquest prompted fierce speculation that she had something to hide. In the 1970s, the *National Times* got hold of her police interviews and published a convoluted story tying her and her husband to the deaths, without taking into account the fact that the couple had a watertight alibi.

Fowler moved to the UK and divorced her husband. Until her own death in 1977, she believed Cold War forces were behind the death of the man she had loved.

The reputations of Ruth and Ken Nash suffered irreparably. Rumours that the party hosts themselves were 'wife-swappers' became cemented in the mythology of the case. Each New Year, they would be reminded of the misery that night had brought to their lives. On New Year's Day, nine years after their fateful party, Ruth Nash died of cancer. Her husband blamed her illness on the stress she suffered because of the Bogle-Chandler affair. An end to the melodrama came on the eleventh anniversary of the Bogle-Chandler deaths, when Ken Nash took a rifle next door to a vacant block and shot himself in the head.

A most unexpected victim was Chief Toxicologist, Vivian Mahoney, who spent more time on the case than anyone else in officialdom. Despite the failed police investigation and the inconclusive Coronial Inquest, Mahoney did not give up on Dr Bogle and Mrs Chandler. He continued searching for the poison that had killed them. A bachelor, Mahoney was in a position to work early mornings and after hours on the case, but every test he carried out produced negative results. In late January 1964, thirteen months after the deaths, he finally ran out of tissue samples:

> That was it. Apart from the blood there was no tissue of any quantity. I left the laboratory about 2.30 in the morning. I'd parked my car right next door to the laboratory. I remember it being very humid and very pressing. And I guess I was tired and threw my coat into the back. I used to drive along Macquarie Street onto the Cahill Expressway, and onto the Sydney Harbour Bridge and I remember turning the case over and over in my mind. It wasn't so much berating myself for failing; I knew I'd given it all I could. I was thinking whether I should have kept some of the sample in case another suggestion came up and you could be in a position to verify it. That's the regret. That's what I was thinking as I was coming onto the Harbour Bridge. And I was very hot, very uncomfortable in the car and I went through the tollgates and I hit the middle of the bridge and stopped the car. I don't think I was fully conscious. I couldn't have been because I got out of the car in the middle of the Harbour Bridge! I sort of wandered around in the bridge area. I felt this rush of air

> and I thought, 'Well that's a nice breeze' and I was walking out into the path of a car. But fortunately a couple of lads, who had followed me in another car, stopped to help me. I just thought there had been an accident and they informed me, 'No, your car is alright.' So they sat with me until about half past three.

Vivian Mahoney had been at the coalface of possibly Australia's greatest mystery. He had single-handedly ruled out many of the 1,000 or so possible causes of death on police records. It was a massive accomplishment, but he took his failure to find the killer poison personally. The morning following his incident on the Harbour Bridge, Vivian Mahoney

Mrs Bogle leaving Australia

resigned his position with the Government Analyst:

> I told Mr Ogg and I said, 'That's it as far as the tissue analysis goes. I've played my last card'. And I said, I'd bring the section up to date with the backlog and then I'd resign. I just wasn't happy with the way things operated. We didn't have as much equipment as we would have liked. The Government Analyst was moving in that direction, but it was a bit too late for the Bogle and Chandler case. So I resigned.

25. Case for the Coroner

In September 2006, Australia's public broadcaster, the ABC, screened my documentary, *Who Killed Dr Bogle & Mrs Chandler?* An estimated 2.5 million people watched the film—a record audience for a documentary on the broadcaster. The next day, hydrogen sulphide was the 'water cooler topic' in workplaces across the country. Radio talkback stations debated the theory and four of the five 'free to air' television stations featured the revelations in their news bulletins.

I had no inkling the film would spark such interest and controversy. Experts were interviewed and most were supportive. But some Bogle Chandler aficionados and retired reporters were disappointed that neither the CIA nor the KGB was to blame. Others expected a murderer to be exposed. That is human nature, I suppose. But until now the public has not been given the full details of the investigation, so it is little wonder conspiracy theories came to fill the void.

To protect public morality and the victims' families, the sexual aspects of the case were covered-up. If the real and obvious purpose behind the couple's liaison at the river had been publicly acknowledged and considered by all the investigators, the enquiry might have led to the conclusion that they were well when they arrived at the river and the poison, therefore, had to be in the vicinity of where they died. Alas, the truth was deemed too salacious for the public good.

The title of the film, *Who Killed Dr Bogle & Mrs Chandler?* was not designed to mislead. In my view, people were responsible for the deaths—namely the owners of the flour and starch company. Despite protestations from their own chemists, they turned the Lane Cove River into an industrial sewer. Societal and governmental indifference to pollution in the 1960s was also a factor.

Today, it is easy to say how environmentally ignorant we were then. But the Lane Cove River still suffers from neglect. As recently as the 1990s, newspapers claimed the river was a 'health hazard'. A scientific study had found pollution levels '88 times higher than the recommended limits'. The Environment Minister advised the public to have 'no contact with the river'. A journalist asked, 'What is being done to save the Lane Cove River? Or is it too late?' At this point, the sewage outfall was still discharging a billion litres of untreated effluent into the waterway every time it rained. In 1997, the head of the Environmental Protection Authority, David Harley, claimed the river had some of the worst sewage overflow problems of any river in the state of New South Wales.[76]

Millions of dollars have since been spent to 'fix' the sewage outfall issue. In 2006, while taking a walk along near where the sewer line crosses the river, I came across a colostomy bag in the mangroves. Fixed indeed! A few metres away, I came across the complete skeleton of a small mammal, also in the mangroves. Recent scientific surveys have shown that while hydrogen sulphide levels in the bottom mud are still higher than one would desire, they are no longer at dangerous levels. Let us hope that remains the case, but the full restoration of the waterway to its glorious pre-industrial state is still just a pipedream. Urban runoff and polluted stormwater continue to degrade the river. The removal of the weir, which effectively cuts the river in two, would allow restoration of the natural tidal flushing. Unfortunately, only the bravest of governments would consider such remedial action. Until then, what was once described as 'a wooing place for lovers' is destined to remain an uninviting drain.

Not everyone will be convinced that the toxic state of the river in 1963 was responsible for the deaths. But to test the theory, one should review the inescapable facts of the case:

- Neither Bogle's or Chandler's worlds were inhabited by criminals, psychopaths or drug-takers.
- There was no evidence to suggest any individual caused the deaths.
- There was no sign of violence on either body.
- The autopsy surgeons found no evidence of a struggle and nothing to suggest murder.
- No person who knew either victim suggested they took illicit drugs or abused prescription drugs.
- No evidence was found in the tissue samples of

either victim of common medications, alcohol, illicit drugs, sexual stimulants or highly toxic compounds.

- The police and the Coroner presented no theory to explain the deaths.
- No person was identified with a real motive to kill the victims.
- Neither victim had a motive to suicide.
- Neither victim had a motive to kill the other.
- No evidence was found to suggest that it was a crime at all.
- Scientific detectives found no drugs or containers used for drugs at any location connected with the victims or people they were associated with.
- The state of undress of the bodies and the pathology reports suggest that the victims were both well when they arrived at the river; so well, in fact, that they were having sex.
- The victims were struck down so suddenly and overwhelmingly that neither was able to correct their clothing.
- Police agencies around the world had not encountered any crime matching these circumstances.
- Britain's leading forensic scientist believed that the victims were gassed.
- There was source of a gas—the bottom of the Lane Cove River.
- Since the late 19th century the river had been a dumping ground for toxic waste, in particular sulphurous waste.

- Since the late 1930s people living beside the river had complained of breathing difficulties and illnesses.
- Millions of fish and eels died as a result of hydrogen sulphide events throughout the 1940s, 50s and 60s.
- A scientific investigation of the river in 1948–49 found hydrogen sulphide gas in explosive and dangerous levels in the river bottom.
- The investigation also discovered the highest concentration of the gas in the bottom mud was within 405 metres of the weir.
- Bogle and Chandler died within 405 metres of the weir.
- Hydrogen sulphide is heavier than air and lingers on the ground in cool air. According to a witness, it was an unseasonably cool evening with mist in the air. Bogle and Chandler arrived at the river at dawn and forensic photos reveal the couple had lain down at water level.
- At high concentrations, hydrogen sulphide overcomes the olfactory nerve in the nose and cannot be detected.
- Recollections of two witnesses at the river that day suggest hydrogen sulphide was present. In one case, a witness walked down to the river at dawn, had breathing difficulties and saw dead fish floating on the surface. The other's dog returned from the river reeking of 'rotten eggs'.
- The waterway was so polluted on New Year's Day that divers were not able to enter it to search for evidence for eleven days.

- The only anomaly found by the Chief Toxicologist was an unusual purplish discolouration of the blood of both victims.
- A purplish discolouration of blood is a fingerprint of hydrogen sulphide poisoning.

In late 2006, I delivered a dossier of my findings to the NSW Police. The report was then forwarded to the Coroner and I awaited a response. After more than four decades, I didn't expect a review of the case to be a priority for one of Australia's busiest Coroners. Soon after, I debated Professor Jo Duflou, the head of Forensic Medicine, on the ABC's television science program *Catalyst*. We were taken to the location beside the river to discuss the hydrogen sulphide theory. Jo Duflou was both charming and sceptical. A few months later, he informed me that the Coroner had handed him my report to review. I assumed that he would knock it on the head overnight.

But on a visit to the United States, he called on Tom Milby, my forensic referee, to discuss the theory. After many hours of debate Tom sensed that Jo Duflou believed the theory was based on circumstantial evidence and unprovable.[61]

While the theory is backed by extensive corroborating documents and testimonies, it is circumstantial. But as I was to discover, there have been many recent cases where circumstantial evidence has resulted in a determination of hydrogen sulphide poisoning.

In New Zealand, at the recent Coronial Inquest into the deaths of Philip Ham and Phillip Binns at Rotorua, the legal team for the Rotorua District Council disputed the implied cause of death from hydrogen sulphide. While they did not challenge the evidence of the toxicologists and pathologists, they claimed that a high 'standard of proof' had not been met. The Coroner disagreed and found that the evidence provided a high level of proof and was satisfied that both men had died as a result of H_2S poisoning.

Tom Milby MD has been an expert witness in numerous legal cases involving hydrogen sulphide poisonings. He believes the evidence presented, most of which was not uncovered by any previous enquiry, should be considered in its entirety:

> If this case were taken to the court, it would be circumstantial in the sense that there is no objective evidence that can be presented. On the other hand, the evidence that we do have is so strong and extremely consistent with hydrogen sulphide related death and I can think of nothing else, neither gas nor any other kind of poison that could argue against that hypothesis. It just seems to me to be unassailable.

Maritime scientist Maurice Fry, who investigated the Lane Cove River's pollution problems in the late 1940s, has no doubts about the soundness of the theory:

> To many people it may seem incredible that the normally delightful River could be so hostile, but the mud analysis reveals the hidden menace. Modern forensic work has produced incontrovertible evidence that Dr Bogle and Mrs Chandler died from hydrogen sulphide poisoning.

> It is regrettable that these unfortunate people were in a hazardous area at the time, when cold air formed a blanketing canopy and coinciding with a sudden release of toxic hydrogen sulphide.

The film has been viewed by numerous environmental scientists, including Professor Julian Crane, who is carrying out a five-year study of the impact of low-level hydrogen sulphide on the populace of Rotorua for the United States National Institute of Health. Professor Crane found the explanation for the deaths 'very convincing'.

In July 2007, Professor Duflou handed his response to the Coroner. It was far more encouraging than I imagined. He stated:

> In my opinion, there is little doubt that both Dr Bogle and Mrs Chandler died as a result of the effects of a poison. There is no evidence of physical trauma to the bodies, and there does not appear to be any evidence of a struggle either from the descriptions of the death scene or at autopsy. Reasonable poisoning options in this case include homicidal poisoning, accidental self-administered poisoning and possibly an environmental poison. To date, no poison has been identified, despite detailed investigations. It appears that neither blood sulphide nor blood thiosulphate levels were assessed at the time. As far as can be ascertained, there is no stored blood available and in my view testing the formalin preserved tissues for these substances would be futile.

> As part of my discussions with Mr Butt and Dr Milby, we considered a number of other drugs and poisons, including the use of amyl nitrite and similar substances as a sexual stimulant. This drug would cause discolouration of the blood (if indeed there was such discolouration), can result in sphincter relaxation and cause pulmonary oedema, but the amount of the drug taken would need to be well in excess of that usually used for recreational purposes. Furthermore, I have also not been able to locate any cases of sudden death as a result of administration of this chemical in previously healthy people.
>
> In conclusion, I am of the opinion that Mr Butt has performed a very thorough investigation of the two deaths, and he has come to a conclusion, which is a reasonable possibility. I recommend he be commended for his excellent work, both as a researcher and as a documentary maker. However, in my view, although his theory remains an entirely reasonable possibility, there is no definite evidence for the proposition he puts forward, and I do not believe further investigations will lead to a definite conclusion.

In many ways it is a positive assessment of the hydrogen sulphide theory. While Professor Duflou did not dismiss any of the scientific or historical evidence presented, he expressed concern about the blood colouration reported to me by toxicologist, Viv Mahoney.

It is certainly peculiar that the toxicologist noted a discolouration and the autopsy pathologist did not. Perhaps at autopsy the blood was drained from the body and sent to the toxicologist as a matter of routine, whereas Mr Mahoney spent considerable time working with the haemoglobin.

Rightly, Jo Duflou questions the 'very long interval between Mr Mahoney performing the investigations and his recall of the blood colour.' But in my conversations with him, he was unequivocal about its strange hue.

Let me again recall the day I met Mahoney at his home. He told me that the Bogle-Chandler investigation was his last major case and that was why he remembered almost every detail. Importantly, I did not mention the H_2S theory or anything of my research until after the interview. The only basis upon which Mahoney agreed to his statement being recorded on film was that he could tell his story without any interruption from me. About fifty minutes into his statement, he mentioned that the only 'odd thing' he found was the blood discolouration.

In our second interview some months later we again discussed blood and the testing method that was available to him at the time:

> Mahoney: Well, I felt it was significant because I hadn't seen it before. That was the main reason. You immediately assume something has changed this colour of the blood other than just not being stored the right way. In fact, it was in both bloods, which ruled out anything in their blood groups. It was quite obvious something had to be consumed or absorbed into the system to change the colour. That wouldn't occur naturally.

Myself: Did you attempt to find the reason for the discolouration of the blood?

Mahoney: There wasn't an all-encompassing scanning method for a blood like there was for anything taken orally. This was the big drawback from the analytical point of view...I tried to analyse the blood myself by a method that I had developed because there was no method of that one at the time, that could do it.

Toxicologist Viv Mahoney was easily the most precise person I have ever interviewed in my thirty years as a filmmaker. His memory was formidable and factually infallible.

Despite his initial resistance to the hydrogen sulphide theory, when he saw the historical evidence I had discovered he came to the opinion that Bogle and Chandler could well have died from exposure to a lethal level of hydrogen sulphide.

I agree with Professor Duflou that now, after almost five decades, it will be impossible to find contemporary evidence to say definitively that Dr Bogle and Mrs Chandler died from hydrogen sulphide poisoning. There are no known surviving blood samples and nothing would be gained from exhuming a body. All we are left with is the historical and scientific evidence presented earlier and the testimonies of the toxicologist and the eyewitness accounts of the people who were at the river that day.

If only there was evidence that other people had died at the river in similar circumstances!

Considering the numerous complaints of local residents over the years, it might seem fortunate that others had not succumbed. As letters to the local council revealed, children experienced breathing difficulties and the council considered evacuating the entire neighbourhood.

The design of the houses along the waterway may explain why residents have not died. Because the Lane Cove River regularly floods, virtually all the dwellings were constructed high off the ground. Concentrations of hydrogen sulphide are highest at ground or water level but diminish considerably with every centimetre.

For humans to die in the open they would certainly have to find themselves in a pool of the gas at ground or water level in still air. The only potential victims one could conceive would be those—like Bogle and Chandler—who ventured down the riverbank and lay down on the mudflats at dawn. We will never know how many other couples did this. The discovery of used condoms and a candle suggests that others had visited the same location some time between Bogle and Chandler's arrival and the previous king-tide. They were very lucky indeed not to have been there at the time of a release of hydrogen sulphide from the river.

If it is a question of luck, Bogle and Chandler were extremely unlucky to be there at the time of a hydrogen sulphide event, as were the bison at Yellowstone National Park and the fishermen on the Japanese lake. Such events are rare. In all these cases, the fatalities occurred due to a convergence of circumstances.

If the gas emissions had occurred half an hour later,

when the sun heated and mixed the air, the fatalities would probably not have occurred. As with a lightning strike or the collapse of a wall that has been standing for centuries, it simply comes down to being in the wrong place at the wrong time.

During its seriously polluted phase, from the 1930s to the 1970s, hundreds of people have died in the river. Most were simple drownings, but how many of these drownings may have been as a result of toxic air?

Take the case of John Morris who was found dead in 1930, in similar circumstances to Dr Bogle and Mrs Chandler. Morris had gone missing two days earlier from his son's home in High Street, Willoughby. A man walking his Beagle dog came across Morris's dead body in scrub beside the Lane Cove River. The police had little to go on. There were no signs of violence. They assumed the man had died of starvation. How a man starved to death after only a few days without food in the middle of a busy city was not explained.

In December 1938, two teenagers died at a Scout Jamboree, located beside Lane Cove River. One fatality was that of a scout who collapsed and died in a portable kitchen beside the river. Two days later, another scout complained of feeling ill just before entering the water for a swim. An hour and a quarter later he was found, drowned. Following the second tragedy, the river was closed to swimmers. Unfortunately, the surviving reports don't offer any explanation as to why either scout died.

The previous year, a Rockdale alderman gave a prescient warning to the Boy Scouts' Association that the Lane Cove River was a risky place to hold its Jamboree. He said the river was 'not healthy. A child's death had been attributed to the condition of the river. There were many dead dogs and cats in it.'

Were any of these cases as a result of hydrogen sulphide? Alas, no police or scientific records survive and the answer remains as elusive as the gas itself.

BOY SCOUTS' JAMBOREE.

Lindfield Site Criticised.

Alderman G. J. McGuire severely criticised the Boy Scouts' Association of New South Wales at the last meeting of Rockdale Council for having selected a site at Lindfield for the jamboree next year. He said that the Lane Cove River, which adjoined the site, was not healthy. A child's death had been attributed to the condition of the river. There were many dead dogs and cats in it.

26. Entwined

The hauntingly beautiful Lane Cove River was the backdrop for one of the world's greatest forensic mysteries—the deaths of Dr Bogle and Mrs Chandler. In the prime of their lives, and with young children, it was a tragic loss for both families. But when investigators failed to find a culprit, the mystery deepened.

In those conservative times, there was no introspection as to what might have driven the victims to seek a momentary escape from their white picket-fence lives in a seedy lovers' lane. At the Coronial Inquest, the mere mention of sex was taboo. Witnesses were stood down and vital evidence was suppressed in the name of 'decency'. Public morality had to be protected.

But at the same time, communication between the police and the scientists was hopelessly compromised. Nobody on the case acknowledged the simple reality that the victims had to have been fit and healthy when they arrived at the river. They could not have been suffering the effects of a poison as they began their 'assignation' on the exposed riverbed on a soft carpet of she-oak needles.

In the absence of any other evidence, it seems extraordinary that investigators did not consider that the obviously polluted state of the waterway could have been linked to the deaths, even though the Police Commissioner himself admitted to the press that its foul state had hampered the investigation.

And so it was that no one even suspected that the lives of the victims and the river itself had become intimately entwined; or that the fate of the lovers was tragically timed to a silent cry from the river, dying.

References

Unacknowledged quotes come from interviews conducted by author or official documents.

1. Bill Jenkings, *As Crime Goes By*, Ironbark Press, p211
2. Interviewed by author, 2005 © Screen Australia
3. Interviewed by author, 2005 © Screen Australia
4. Interviewed by author, 2005 © Screen Australia
5. Australian Dictionary of Biography: Bogle, Gilbert Stanley http://adbonline.anu.edu.au/biogs/A130243b.htm
6. National Archives of Australia, Dr. G. S. Bogle CSIRO employment file, A8520 PH/BOG/004
7. National Archives of Australia, Dr. G. S. Bogle CSIRO employment file, A8520 PH/BOG/004
8. p2, *Sun* 7 January 1963
9. Geoffrey Chandler, *So You think I Did It!*, Sun Books
10. Interviewed by author, 2005 © Screen Australia
11. Geoffrey Chandler, *So You think I Did It!*, Sun Books
12. Interviewed by author, 2005 © Screen Australia
13. Interviewed by author, 2005 © Screen Australia
14. Interviewed by author, 2005 © Screen Australia
15. Interviewed by author, 2005 © Screen Australia
16. Interviewed by author, 2005 © Screen Australia
17. Stafford Silk, *The Bogle Mystery*, p13
18. Alex Mitchell, p64 *Come the Revolution*, UNSW Press
19. Interviewed by author, 2005 © Screen Australia
20. Interviewed by author, 2005
21. Interviewed by author, 2005 © Screen Australia
22. Interviewed by author, 2005 © Screen Australia
23. Interviewed by author, 2005 © Screen Australia
24. Bill Jenkings, *As Crime Goes By*, Ironbark Press
25. Bruce Swanton and retired Inspector Lance Hoban, The story of Norman Thos. William Allan
26. Bill Jenkings, *As Crime Goes By*, Ironbark Press
27. p3, *Sunday Mirror*, 6 January, 1963
28. Interviewed by author, 2005 © Screen Australia
29. Marian Wilkinson, 'Bogle Chandler: The Untold Story', *National Times*, 15-18 August, 1982
30. Interviewed by author, 2005 © Screen Australia
31. Interviewed by author, 2005 © Screen Australia
32. Letter P. Lesley Bidstrup to Prof John Cleland, 6 March, 1969

33. Letter John Laing, Director of Forensic Medicine to Prof John Cleland, 3 May, 1966
34. There have been no recorded cases of 1080 causing harm to human health, let alone any deaths of humans due to 1080 poisoning. Long-term, low-level exposure is not harmful – tea drinkers consume 1080 at about 1.5 times the drinking water limit with every cup of ordinary tea. All over the world millions of people have been regularly consuming 1080 for centuries with no discernible ill effects.
35. Letter Prof John Cleland to McCarthy, Poisons Branch, SA Dept Public Health, 1969
36. Letter Prof John Cleland to McCarthy, Poisons Branch, SA Dept Public Health, 1969
37. Letter John Cleland to Inspector of Police, May 1969
38. Letter John Cleland to Norman Allan, Commissioner of Police, 28 April, 1969
39. Letter L.F. Newman, Ass. Commissioner of Police to J.B. Cleland, 12 May, 1969.
40. Letter John Laing, Director of Forensic Medicine to Prof John Cleland, 21 Feb, 1964
41. Cameron Hazlehurst, Australian Dictionary of Biography http://www.adb.online.anu.edu.au/biogs/A130626b.htm
42. *The Daily Mirror* 7 Aug 1984, p1
43. National Archives of Australia, CHANDLER, Jeffrey Arnold and CHANDLER, Mrs M [Margaret] and BOGLE, Dr G [Gilbert], Control symbol 1963/520, pp 20-21
44. David McKnight, *Australia's Spies and Their Secrets*, p 10
45. Minutes a leaked British Cabinet Meeting on 8 July 1948
46. http://en.wikipedia.org/wiki/History_of_LSD
47. http://en.wikipedia.org/wiki/History_of_LSD
48. http://www.a1b2c3.com/drugs/lsd05.htm
49. Michael Blumenfield, James J. Strain, *Psychosomatic Medicine: Principals and Practice* p471
50. Interviewed by author 2005 © Screen Australia
51. Lane Cove Municipal Council Correspondence series 1920-1960 File 218, Lane Cove Library
52. Lane Cove Municipal Council Correspondence series 1920-1960 File 218, Lane Cove Library
53. Lane Cove Municipal Council Correspondence series 1920-1960 File 218, Lane Cove Library
54. Lane Cove Municipal Council Correspondence series 1920-1960 File 218, Lane Cove Library

55. Interviewed by author 2005 © Screen Australia
56. L. McLoughlin, *Middle Lane Cove River: History and Future*
57. Investigation on 'pollution of Lane Cove River' 1948 by M.D. Fry, Maritime Services Board of NSW
58. Report, Royal Comission Noxious Trades, p6.
59. Beverley Johnson *The Corngrinder*, p53
60. Interviewed by author 2006
61. M.D Fry, Investigation on Pollution of Lane Cove River 1948, p1
62. 'Let Us ALL Keep Our Harbour Clean' *The Sunday Herald* (Sydney, NSW : 1949-1953) Sunday 11 January 1953 p2
63. *Middle Lane Cove River: History and a Future*, Lynne McLoughlin p62
64. *Sydney Morning Herald* 21 Nov 1968 p6
65. Kyle Tennant, *Sydney Morning Herald* 22 August, 1953 p7
66. Interviewed by author 2005 © Screen Australia
67. Brian Lane, *The Encyclopedia of Forensic Science* p97, 98
68. Clinical Toxicology of Commercial Products: Acute Poisoning.
69. Reference: NSW Police 1971 Toxicology review Bogle-Chandler Case, L.G. Clark
70. *Forensic Science International* Volume 66, Issue 2, 3 June 1994, pp111-116
71. Rare Combination Of Events Cause Of Bison Deaths In Yellowstone National Park, Yellowstone National Park News Release March 23, 2004
72. AW Freireich MD Hydrogen Sulphide Poisoning Report of Two Cases, On Fatal Outcome from Associated Mechanical Asphyxia AM J Path 22: 147-150, 1946
73. Brian Makrell, Rotorua's Silent Serial Killer, *Investigate* Dec 2000 pp 46-50
74. Inquest Into The Deaths Of Philip John Ham And Phillip Stanley Binns, Coroner Dr Wallace Bain P14
75. *Sydney Morning Herald*, Wednesday 3 January 1906, p8
76. *North Shore Times* May 16, 1997

PHOTOGRAPHS & DOCUMENTS

1. New Year's Day

Dr Bogle's Car - courtesy George Lindsay

Dr Bogle – scene from *Who Killed Dr Bogle & Mrs Chandler?*, courtesy National Film and Sound Archive/ Rhys Muldoon

Body under cardboard – scene from *Who Killed Dr Bogle &*

Mrs Chandler?, courtesy National Film and Sound Archive

2. Alibi

Geoffrey Chandler – courtesy George Lindsay

Pamela Logan - Mitchell Library, State Library of NSW – Witness in the Bogle-Chandler case, Central Court Australian Photographic Agency – 14141

3. The Victims

Dr Gilbert Bogle – courtesy Doug Milne

Dr Bogle in his laboratory – courtesy John Sierens

Margaret Chandler – source unknown

The Chandlers – courtesy Geoffrey Chandler

Margaret and Geoffrey Chandler – courtesy Geoffrey Chandler

5. Autopsies

Government Analyst Laboratory – courtesy John Plowman

Toxicology Laboratory – courtesy John Plowman/Vivian Mahoney

6. A Room Full of Suspects

Dr Bogle's artwork – George Lindsay

7. Motive For Murder

Police Running Sheet – courtesy NSW Police

Evidence collected - courtesy George Lindsay

Toxicology document – courtesy George Lindsay

8. Poison

Nash Home – courtesy George Lindsay

9. Bitter Pill

Sheridan Pausey – permission Dr S. Pausey

Mrs Chandler and dachshunds © Cummings/Fairfax Syndication

10. Tabloid War

Weird Cults – *Sunday Telegraph* January 20, 1963, p1

Death Dress – *Sun*, January 17, 1963, p1 Fairfax Syndication

Dr Bogle's Death Ray – *Australian Scientist* Vol 1, Number 3 - April 1961

11. Lady Killer

Dr Bogle with staff – courtesy John Sierens

Margaret Fowler – Mitchell Library, State Library of NSW, Bogle-Chandler inquest, Coroner's Court, Sydney Australian Photographic Agency -14170

Bogle's Affair with his Killer – *Daily Mirror*, October 19, 1982 p1

12. Third Person

Bush Track - courtesy George Lindsay Bush Track - courtesy George Lindsay

Bush Track - courtesy George Lindsay Bush Track - courtesy George Lindsay

13. Inquest

Geoffrey Chandler - Mitchell Library, State Library of NSW, Mr. Chandler, Bogle-Chandler case, Central Court Australian Photographic Agency – 14136

Coroner Jack Loomes - Mitchell Library, State Library of NSW, Personalities, Bogle-Chandler inquest, Coroner's Court, Sydney Australian Photographic Agency - 13864

Sergeant Goode assisting the Coroner - Mitchell Library, State Library of NSW, Personalities, Bogle-Chandler inquest,

Coroner's Court, Sydney Australian Photographic Agency - 13866

Pamela Logan arrives at the Inquest - Mitchell Library, State Library of NSW, Witnesses in the Bogle-Chandler case, Central Court Australian Photographic Agency – 14169

Strangers May Suffer –*Sun*, May 27, 1963

Ruth and Ken Nash - © Jim Rice/Fairfax Syndication

14. Red Herring

Conus geographus – courtesy Rokus Groeneveld

15. Conspiracy

Dr Bogle in his laboratory – courtesy Doug Milne

CSIRO Building which housed Bogle and Chandler's laboratories – Peter Butt

FBI Director, J. Edgar Hoover - http://www.fbi.gov/news/photos

Letter to J. Edgar Hoover – Courtesy NSW Police

16. The Watcher

Chandler and his lawyer, Kevin Murray © B Mullaney/Fairfax Syndication

18. Sole Witness

Fairyland, Lane Cove River - Mitchell Library, State Library of NSW - a105455

Mangroves – © Peter Butt

Fairyland, Lane Cove River - Mitchell Library, State Library of NSW - a105456

Fullers Bridge – courtesy Maurice Fry

Water sampling - courtesy Maurice Fry

Maurice Fry - courtesy Maurice Fry

River Pollution a Worry to Homes – *Sun*, 30 Aug 1947

Chicago Mills - Mitchell Library, State Library of NSW - a105462

Tom Milby MD – © Peter Butt

Map – Peter Butt

20. The Case Files

Dr Francis Camps – unknown

Victim's clothing – courtesy George Lindsay

Mrs Chandler's shoes – courtesy George Lindsay

Poisons – courtesy NSW Police

20. Fingerprint

Viv Mahoney – courtesy V. Mahoney

23. Dark Secret

Eddy Batiste with champion greyhound – National Greyhound News *National Greyhound News* cover - National Greyhound News

24. Damage

Mrs Bogle Leaves Australia © Fairfax Syndication

25. Case for the Coroner

Boy Scouts Jamboree – *Sydney Morning Herald*, Monday 12 July 1937, p6

26. Entwined

Dr Bogle and Mrs Chandler at the river - scene from *Who Killed Dr Bogle & Mrs Chandler?*, courtesy National Film and Sound Archive/ Rhys Muldoon, Octavia Barron-Martin

PETER BUTT began making films in the early 1980s. After successfully securing the Australian cinema release of his first film, *No Such a Place*, alongside Peter Weir's *Gallipoli*, Peter has continued to produce documentary films for international and Australian broadcasters.

Over the past decade Peter has focused on uncovering new information about Australia's Cold War history. His films include:

- *Silent Storm*, which uncovers secret animal and human experiments carried out during the British atomic tests.
- *Fortress Australia*, which reveals Australia's secret attempts to acquire nuclear weapons.
- *Lies, Spies and Olympics*, which explores the impact of the Cold War on the 1956 Melbourne Olympics.
- *The Prime Minister is Missing*, which uncovers new evidence about the disappearance of Harold Holt.
- *I, Spry*, which brings to light the early days of ASIO.
- Peter's 2006 film *Who Killed Dr Bogle & Mrs Chandler?* won a Logie Award, a Critics' Circle Award and a Walkley Award nomination.